HOLD ON
TO
YOUR
DREAMS

HOLD ON TO YOUR DREAMS

Regardless of Your Past

Françoise Maricle

Hold On to Your Dreams: Regardless of Your Past
Published by Dream Write Design
Whiting, New Jersey, U.S.A.

Maricle, Françoise, Author
Hold On to Your Dreams
Françoise Maricle

Library of Congress Control Number: 2025907271

ISBN: 979-8-9928936-0-1, 979-8-9928936-1-8 (paperback)
ISBN: 979-8-9928936-2-5 (digital)

Editing: Constance Monroe (monroecoaching.com)
Print & Digital Book Design: Amit Dey (amitdey2528@gmail.com)
Publishing Management: Susie Schaefer (finishthebookpublishing.com)

BIOGRAPHY & AUTOBIOGRAPHY / Women
FAMILY & RELATIONSHIPS / Family History & Genealogy
HISTORY / Wars & Conflicts / World War II / Pacific Theater
SOCIAL SCIENCE / Emigration & Immigration

QUANTITY PURCHASES: Schools, companies, professional groups, clubs, and other organizations may qualify for special terms when ordering quantities of this title. For information, email cjmonroeconsulting@gmail.com

DEDICATION

"Dedicated to the Allied liberators of the
Dutch East Indies whose courage and compassion
brought freedom to those in captivity.

I would not be here today without them.

For my late husband Gary. Thank you for our beautiful
life together and for encouraging me to write this book."

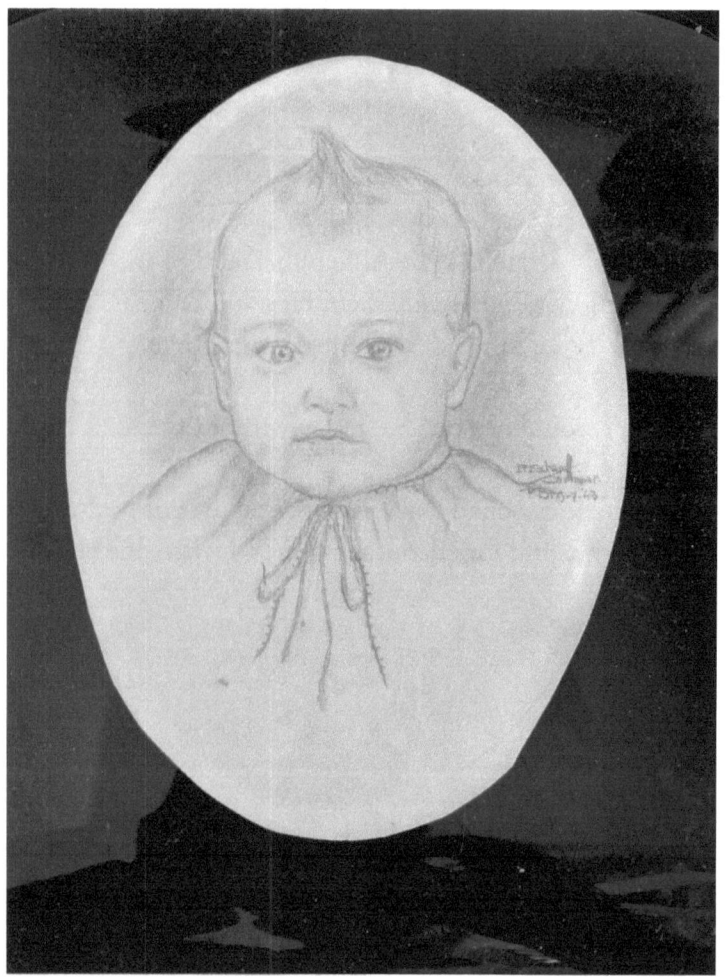

The only image of me as a baby thanks to one of our friends in the camp.

WHY I WROTE THIS BOOK

When I first published this book in 2007, it was a major accomplishment for me. It took me seven years to write it because every time I tried to write, I felt this unbearable heavy load in my mind and in my heart just thinking about all the horrible experiences that I had endured when I came into the world. After about five or so years of writing and rewriting, my darling husband Gary finally said to me "either finish writing it or delete the whole thing." I don't know if it was because he saw me struggling or if he just wanted me to stop thinking about it, but I thought it was good advice. His persuasion certainly got me to finally publish my manuscript.

My main purpose in writing this book in the first place was because whomever I shared my life story with, did not know that there was a Japanese War Camp in Indonesia during World War II for non-native people from all over the world living there. These were people like my father, mother, brother and me. These camps were just as horrific as the Nazi camps into which Jewish people were forced and which are very well known and documented.

The page to the left is a sketch of me as a baby. This is the only image of me at that age since I was born in the camp and there were no cameras to be found. The fact that I survived those horrible surroundings was a miracle in and of itself. The woman who sketched me could have been killed if she was found with the pencil and paper she used to sketch my image. After she gave the sketch to my mother, my mother could have been killed as well. That is just one of the awful things that people experienced in the Nazi camps. As you read about the camp where I was born, you will see more similarities between what my family and I did to survive and what Jewish survivors have reported.

The relaunch of this book isn't proving to be any easier for me, as I've had to rethink everything that was included in the original version. Of course, I was very young when we were liberated from the camp, so I have absolutely no memory of the day-to-day living there, but there are certain situations that still make me uncomfortable to this day. For example, I do not like windows which have a lot of square windowpanes. I don't know if I ever saw windows like that when I was in the camp, but I think they remind me of barbed wires and that type of image makes me feel like I'm in prison. One of the homes I moved into with Gary had this type of window in it and I made him remove the windows because of this. They were perfectly good windows, but I insisted that Gary remove the windows and replace them with something less disturbing to me.

Another issue for me is that I could never stay anywhere with no sound or no light. I think this is because in the camp it was very dark and very quiet. To this day I sleep with the TV on all night long because the light and sound from the TV makes me feel safe.

In the early days of being in the camp, my mother discovered she was pregnant with me but because my parents were separated into the required "male" and "female" camps, my father never even knew I was born until after the war. Imagine his surprise when he met me! I remember him being a very distant father figure. This was one of many situations where I could feel my parents' anguish over how we had been living in the camp, and as a child I just knew it wasn't normal. My motivation to do a relaunch is more than just getting this part of history told; it is about the 80th anniversary of liberation which will happen on August 15th of 2025. Even though I was almost three years old and don't have any memory of liberation day, I want my book to honor all the survivors in the camp where I was born as well as the brave soldiers who set us free, and make sure that they are all celebrated the same way all the other survivors throughout history are celebrated when these big milestones occur.

Another reason to relaunch my story is because a lot has happened in my own life since the original publication. My readers often ask what happened after I first published this book, and I'd like to fill in the blanks for them. My dear husband Gary passed away on February 8th, 2020, right before the COVID pandemic officially started on 3/11/2020, and caused the US to pretty much shut down. It was also just 10 days before our 56th wedding anniversary, and it was devastating for me. I lost twenty pounds in two-three months, and I felt depressed for a very long time.

Eventually Gary's words came to haunt me. He always said, "If I die before you, I want you to live your life and be happy." Once again, my dear Gary provided some good advice. In the end I thought to myself: "I had two choices: either feel sorry for myself and wallow in my sadness, or I could start over."

In between the time when I first published this book in 2007 and Gary's death in 2020, Gary and I traveled to many places in the United States in our motor home. We have been to every state in the USA except for New York, and those states north of New York. We even drove through Canada to get to Alaska where our daughter lives. We volunteered in Arches National Park and the Petrified Forest for several years. Gary and I also went on our first cruise during those years. We cruised out of San Diego to Hawaii, and liked Hawaii so much that we went back on a longer vacation! We also did some international travel and visited my family in the Netherlands. I also went back to Indonesia. The only place Gary would not agree to go to was New York City. He thought that a trip to New York would have been just too dangerous.

Here I am four years after Gary's death back traveling again. Gary might not be with me physically, but I know he is following my footsteps from the other side. I'm certain that my recent trips to Florida,

Las Vegas, a cruise to the Caribbean and two trips to Alaska would have gained his stamp of approval. One of my next trips might not be so pleasing to him. However, I have decided, it's time for me to go to New York City and fulfill my lifelong dream of seeing the Statue of Liberty and Ellis Island. When I first came to the States it was by plane. I landed in New York City, but was only there briefly because I had to change planes to fly to Chicago and then on to Iowa. I did all this traveling in one trip with my new born baby in tow. In addition, I had very little knowledge of the English language, and no help from anyone! I have heard so many immigration stories from people coming through Ellis Island and seeing that great symbol of freedom "Lady Liberty," that I have always thought it would be an amazing place to experience firsthand.

Many times, when a person celebrates a big birthday in the U.S., they are presented with a "Remember When" birthday card. It takes you back to the year you were born and presents you with all kinds of facts about that year: I.E., the average cost of purchasing a home, what the most popular car was to drive, who was the number one song writer that year, who won the Oscar for best actor, etc. When I think about what was going on around me when I was born in Indonesia, I'd rather not see what would be in that card, and prefer to think about how I envisioned my life as I grew older. I imagined traveling worldwide, and one day living in the United States, in a house with a yard.

More importantly, I wanted to feel free and leave my terrible beginnings behind in Indonesia, in that horrific Japanese war camp where they belonged. I was determined to have a happy life, one without so much worry and fear. Thankfully I met Gary, my handsome American husband who wanted many of the same things that I did. I am a living example of how it pays off to hold onto your dreams regardless of your past. If you can imagine a better future, you can achieve it as well.

CHAPTER 1

My mom, Teuna, and dad, Francois, both citizens of the Netherlands, were living in Indonesia before World War II broke out. Indonesia, also known as the Dutch East Indies, was a colony of the Netherlands. Enterprising Dutch people immigrated to Indonesia because life was so much more comfortable there than in the Netherlands. There just wasn't any comparison between the two countries, especially for the adventurous at heart.

Tropical Indonesia had no cold, damp winters or summers that fluctuated from being warm for a few days, then cold and dreary, and then warm again like they often were in the Netherlands. The temperature didn't vary much from summer to winter, but they did have a wet season and a dry season. During the wet season it could become very humid which was not always comfortable for some people, but they lived in such a way that they weren't too uncomfortable most of the time.

The sun was shining most every day, the monsoon rains never lasted long, and the sun was often still shining while it rained. Everyone took siestas in the afternoon when it was too hot to work. This left everyone rested up and ready for an evening of fun and relaxation. Children went to school early in the morning and were home in time to eat lunch. The younger ones took naps while the older ones had quiet time in their rooms. After it cooled down everyone showered and continued with their day.

There was no land or housing shortage and everybody lived in spacious homes with large, beautifully landscaped gardens, so much different from the small apartments most people occupied in the Netherlands.

The whole lifestyle in Indonesia was relaxed and easy. Young children were allowed to play outside without worry and have a carefree childhood. They learned very early in life that certain animals and insects in the jungle needed to be left alone. There was no immediate danger if they stayed where they were told to be and romped around in the safe areas.

However, it wasn't a perfect place by any means. Children sometimes had to go to boarding school because most schools were too distant to attend on a daily basis. And when they went on to high school, they were often sent to the Netherlands because the education was much better there. This meant that they were away from their families for long periods of time.

My father managed a rubber plantation for the Dutch government on the island of Sumatra. Sumatra is one of about 13,000 islands that make up Indonesia and is one of the biggest islands. He liked his job even though it meant that he had to put in long days, but he worked outdoors on a beautiful island. He remembered the days at work in the Netherlands where he was sitting in an office and staring at a dreary sky and buildings wherever he looked. His responsibility in Indonesia was supervising the clearing of the jungle and the planting of rubber trees. Controlled fires would be set in areas that needed clearing and then new trees were planted. He really enjoyed being outside even though it was hot and humid and he wasn't raised in that kind of climate. He liked the vastness of the land and the relative job freedom he had.

My mother, who was born on the island of Sumatra, liked the climate as well but didn't necessarily like living so far from civilization. She would rather have lived closer to her friends and acquaintances so that they could visit back and forth. Shopping was not easy because of the distance away from the nearest town and wasn't done too often.

And mail was only delivered once every three weeks or so. But she still liked living there better than in cold, gray Holland. She had lived in the Netherlands while growing up and getting her education there.

Living on a tropical island had other advantages. There were always plenty of fresh and varied kinds of fruits and vegetables. The fruits were ripened to perfection on the trees or bushes before they were picked to be eaten. I never understood why my father complained about the fruit we bought at the store in the Netherlands. Later in life, when I was able to pick ripe oranges and grapefruits from the tree or diverse berries from the bushes, I knew what he was talking about. There is just no comparison in taste between tree-ripened and store-bought fruit.

The chickens ran around the courtyard pecking at whatever they could find to eat and their eggs were brought in every morning right after they were laid. When chickens were slaughtered and cooked, the meat was firm and tasty, unlike the watery, flabby chickens found in grocery stores today. All the food was of very high quality and everything was fresh, delicious, and plentiful.

My parents also had a home in the mountains where they vacationed, spent long weekends, or stayed whenever it got too hot for them on the plantation. There were no air-conditioners in the 1930s and it did get humid in the jungle when a monsoon hit.

We were also fortunate to have an automobile; a veritable luxury in those days. Even my mother could drive a car; she was very proud of being able to drive the big Buick they had. She was quite ahead of her time in that respect. My dad didn't have to do any maintenance on the car as he had a mechanic who kept it in perfect running condition. and a "boy" who kept it washed. A "boy" wasn't necessarily a young person but anybody who was a male servant was called a "boy."

My parents entertained whenever they wanted. The full-time servants helped them prepare everything for those parties and clean up afterwards. My mother didn't have to do anything but tell the staff what meal menu she wanted and what needed to be done each day. My father loved to give parties and play practical jokes on people, but more about that later. However, most of the parties took place in town at the "Soos," which was the social club for the Europeans.

They were allowed vacations every six years to return to the Netherlands and sailed there in luxury by cruise ship. It took six weeks to get to the Netherlands and six weeks to return to Indonesia. Their total leave was six months which gave them plenty of time to visit with family and friends and to see other parts of their country or neighboring countries.

This is the kind of life I could have had. Quite often I dream of what my life would have been like if I had been raised under those conditions. It seems like a fairy tale, and I often wished that things could have continued that way. Unfortunately, I wasn't destined for that kind of life.

CHAPTER 2

On March 8, 1942 the Japanese invaded Sumatra. The invasion didn't come as a total surprise to the inhabitants. They knew the Japanese were already invading other areas and were coming closer and closer to Indonesia. It was a well-known fact that the Japanese had started invading portions of China in the 1930's and slowly, but surely, they had come closer and closer to the Indonesian island of Sumatra.

The day after the Japanese attacked Pearl Harbor in 1941 my dad got called up for service in the KNIL, even though he was 44 years old. KNIL stands for Koninklijk Nederlands-Indisch Leger which means Royal Dutch-Indonesian Service. The KNIL was formed to fight off attacks by the Indonesian people and had been in existence since the early 1800s. Life in paradise came to a quick halt. He was not allowed to tell anyone where he was stationed. Sometime in January of 1942 my mother received a telephone call informing her that she and my brother Ton had to go to Medan where she would be able to spend a short time with my dad. And then once more they were able to spend some time together in late February or early March. It was during that time I was conceived. Shortly thereafter my dad was sent away, and he and my mom didn't hear from each other or see each other until December of 1945.

After the Japanese attacked Pearl Harbor, they invaded the Philippines and the peninsula of Malakka. On December 25, 1941, Hong Kong was invaded, on January 2, 1942, Manila was invaded. On

January 10, 1942, the Japanese invasion of Kalimantan, Sulawesi, and Ambon began. During the Battle of the Java Sea that lasted from February 27 until March 1, 1942, the Japanese destroyed the allied fleet and the invasion of Java started. On February 15, 1942, Singapore was invaded. On March 8, 1942, the Dutch people on Java had to surrender. The remainder of the soldiers of the KNIL became prisoners of war after the capitulation.

Up until March 8, 1942, the colonialists didn't comprehend the great danger they would soon be in. They were expecting the Japanese to come by sea; therefore, the Dutch, English, Germans, Australians and others who lived there had all the harbors guarded as securely as possible and were ready for the Japanese arrival. They were positive that they were well prepared and could wipe out the Japanese invasion in a relatively short time. In fact, the majority was so sure that they could defeat the Japanese very quickly that they didn't send their wives and children back to Europe or Australia. After all, Europe was already in the midst of the war against the Germans. They believed that their families would be safer in Indonesia.

You might ask why the Japanese would want to take over the thousands of islands of Indonesia? I've been told that the sole reason was because of the abundant resources available there. The Japanese desperately needed them, especially oil and rubber, for use in conquering other parts of the Pacific. With these natural resources they could become a very strong country and eventually subdue the entire Pacific.

In the beginning of March, 1942, airplanes were heard overhead. The people on the islands still weren't alarmed as airplanes flew over Indonesia all the time on their way to Australia. But once they took a closer look at the planes, they discovered that these planes were unfamiliar. To their horror they realized they were Japanese warplanes. They quickly realized that it would now be nearly impossible to escape.

Soon the airplanes landed at nearby airports or on landing strips. Out of the planes came the Japanese all ready for their mission. Paratroopers descended from the sky. Where they landed depended on what area the soldiers wanted to take over. They were well prepared and knew exactly where they wanted to go to.

If they wanted to capture people who lived in a rural area, they parachuted in close to the plantations. Then they marched right up to the inhabitants' houses or cycled up on fold-up bicycles that were attached to their backs.

The Japanese rode their bikes up to the houses where my parents and other colonialists lived and informed them in no uncertain terms that war had begun. They said they would return for them in 24 hours and that they must leave their houses and all their belongings behind. They were told to be ready the next day and that the only things they could take with them were whatever they could carry. They were also instructed to carry their belongings themselves as nobody was going to transport anything for them.

Everything else had to be left behind with the full knowledge that, most likely, they would never see their possessions again. Some people buried their belongings in the yard behind their house in the hopes of getting them back when the war was over. It is hard to imagine the turmoil people went through not only because of the valuables left behind but not knowing what was going to happen to them, and how long the Japanese were going to keep them captive. The takeover of the remainder of Indonesia followed quickly.

There was no way to escape from the islands, as the people who tried soon found out. Many people gathered their most valuable possessions, identification papers, gold, jewelry and a few pieces of clothing and boarded any available boat or ship in an attempt to flee to Australia or elsewhere. Most of them died as the Japanese bombed their boats shortly after they left the harbor. Any survivors who were able to swim ashore were greeted by the Japanese who captured them. They soon found out what happened if they showed any resistance. Anyone trying to run away was shot and killed or beaten so badly that they wished they were dead. Women and children witnessed their loved ones being executed or brutally beaten. They quickly realized they shouldn't defend their husbands, fathers, or family members or they risked the same fate. They weren't even allowed to say goodbye to their loved ones or to even spend a moment or two with a dead loved one. The Japanese favored no one.

Hiding on the islands was almost impossible unless you were very familiar with the jungle, knew what foods to eat safely, and where to hide without being attacked by jungle animals. If you hid in the jungle and the Indonesian people found you, they would turn you over to the Japanese. The Japanese soldiers had quickly befriended the Indonesian people. They had won them over by telling them that they would help them be free from the Dutch if they cooperated with the Japanese. The Indonesian people desperately wanted their independence and were willing to do whatever the Japanese told them to do.

On that dreadful day, the Japanese came back to take us to the camps. The women carried many things including some toys for the smaller children. The bigger children carried whatever they could. It was quite an exodus. All the men and boys 12 years of age and older were put in camps separate from the women and younger children. Younger boys who looked 12 years or older, and couldn't prove they weren't 12 yet, were sent to the men's camps and separated from their mothers. The goodbyes were very quick and very emotional as nobody knew where the others were going and how long it would be before they would see them again, if ever.

About 60,000 children were interned during the war including children who, like me, were born during the internment. On that horrible day in March 1942, my father, who was almost 45, was shipped to a far-off destination. My 28-year-old mother, and my brother, Ton, who was almost five, went to the first camp not far from where they had originally lived.

My mother, brother, and I were in three different camps during the war, each one worse than the one before. All the camps were near towns and were named after them. The first camp was near Pulau Brayan the nicest place we stayed during the war. This camp wasn't very far from where we lived before the war broke out and consisted of beautiful, spacious houses previously owned by the white colonialists. Barbed wire fences to detain the people now surrounded this area of lovely homes. All the furniture and other items in these homes had been stolen by the Japanese or Indonesian people, except for some mattresses that were put on the floor. How sadly different the inside of the houses looked without furniture and nothing hanging on the walls. The rooms were occupied according to their size. Each person was allotted a small amount of space. The bigger the room, the more people who would share it. There were nine people in the room we had. This was not an ideal situation by any means, especially not once I was born, but the other rooms in the house were equally crowded.

The second camp was near the town Glugur, and the third one near Aik Paminke. Each successive move was deeper into the jungle and farther away from civilization which made it that much harder to escape. Each new camp was also less habitable.

Sometimes the men's and women's camps were not very far apart, so husbands and wives were able to occasionally see each other through the fence or hear from others how their loved ones were doing. The Japanese assigned the men a variety of labor to do. On their march to and from where they were needed, they occasionally would see the women briefly and very carefully give them a message orally, or on a small scrap of paper. This was very dangerous to do though and could result in severe punishment if the Japanese were to see it happen.

At other times the camps were hundreds of miles apart and across a body of water, as was the case with my mother and father. My father, who was almost 45 years old and quite gray, was sent to Burma where the internees worked on the railroad and the famous bridge over the River Kwai. My mom and dad certainly tried to keep in contact with each other during the duration of the war, but their letters and other messages somehow never reached each other.

At the time of the Japanese invasion, my parents didn't know yet that my mother was pregnant. As soon as she found out for certain, she tried to send a message to my father. He never received it which turned out to be very detrimental for me, as you will learn later.

My mother normally carried her baby full term, but this time it would be different. The circumstances she was in, combined with the stress and the lack of proper nutrition, took its toll. She felt that things weren't going right, so she wanted to deliver her baby in the hospital outside the camp where the baby's survival chances would be much better than if she delivered in the camp. After all, there would be doctors and nurses at the hospital who would know what to do with a newborn baby. There were no doctors and only one nurse in the camp, and my mother had very limited, if any, ways of taking care of me. She also knew that her baby would have a better chance for survival if it were kept for a time in the hospital after the delivery. The hospital staff would know how to deliver a baby, take care of it properly, keep it warm, and would have the means to do so. Even though we lived in the tropics, a baby, especially a premature one, needed to be kept warm at night as the air temperature dropped drastically after the sun went down.

The Japanese initially refused her request to deliver her baby at the hospital. My parents, however, were good friends of the president of the company for whom my father worked. He, in turn, was a friend of the administrator of the hospital in Medan, as well as a friend of a physician who knew the administrator. My mother explained to him that she was worried that she was going to deliver prematurely. She didn't want to lose this baby as she had already lost a baby boy. That boy, her second child, had died when he was about a year old. She very much wanted to make sure that her care would be better during the delivery than if she stayed in the camp where she would have to rely on strangers for help.

One day, to the total surprise of my mother, a Japanese guard told her to report to the office. She didn't know what to expect but went immediately. She was told to bring all her belongings and report with my brother to the gate at a certain time and be ready to go to the hospital. For some unknown reason the guards let them go that particular day. The reason for bringing all their belongings was because one was never sure of returning to the same place.

I was born two months prematurely on September 18, 1942, and only weighed about four pounds at birth. Because of my low birth weight, my mother and I were allowed to stay in the hospital until I weighed almost five pounds. In the early 1940s, and certainly during the war, hospitals weren't equipped for premature babies — at least not like they are now. There were no special machines to keep me breathing, no modern facilities, and not even particularly hygienic conditions. However, while we were in the hospital my mother was able to put a hot water bottle in my crib to keep my body temperature more or less constant.

While my mother was in the hospital, my brother played with other children who were also there. For a short time, his life improved somewhat as well. He received better food and care than before. For a brief time, he was out of the grim surroundings of the last six months and that he would be in for the next three years.

Soon we had to go back to the camp as other patients needed the room, care, and attention. My mother tried her hardest to keep us in the hospital a little longer, hoping that I could gain a little more weight before being sent back to the camp. But even my mother's friend's influence couldn't keep us there any longer.

The prospects for my survival, of course, were minimal. I no longer had a warm water bottle to keep me warm, nor were the cleaner conditions in the hospital available in the camp. The camp was far from clean and safe. Also, I couldn't tolerate my mother's milk which she then gave to a baby whose mother hadn't enough. Whenever possible my mother got a special, easier to digest milk for me. Later, if I could tolerate it, I got a little rice or some of the foods other people ate. Most of the time, my tiny body couldn't absorb the garbage given to us. This caused me to grow and develop very slowly, barely keeping me alive.

I didn't sleep very well from birth. Consequently, I was awake a lot, needing to be fed and cared for. For a short time, my mother was able to keep the three of us in a very small kitchen. There was just enough room for two mattresses; one for her and my brother, and my little bed, which was actually a small basket. She kept the basket off the cold floor by setting it on the stove, that before the war, had been used for cooking meals. Even in the tropics concrete floors can get very cold at night, depending on the time of the year.

Prenatal care, postnatal care, or any medical care for that matter, was unavailable unless it was done by a doctor, nurse or midwife who happened to be interned as well. There were no doctors in the camps we were in. The Red Cross medications meant for us were only distributed by the Japanese to the Japanese. After all, they needed to be strong to win the war! Just like the Germans, they believed they were the super race.

Prisoners were told there were no medical supplies for them no matter how much they begged and pleaded with their Japanese captors. After the war was over, rooms full of stockpiled medications were found. Many lives could have been saved, and many illnesses shortened, if the medications had been properly distributed. Sadly, there probably was enough medication for all of us, including the Japanese.

The food rations initially distributed to us consisted of less than half the total calories needed for the average adult to exist on. The shortage of fat, vitamins, minerals, and proteins in our diet caused a variety of deficiencies making people more susceptible to infections, a multiplicity of diseases, and to become bloated, an ironic side effect of starvation.

The bloating didn't occur just in the bellies. Some people became so bloated that they couldn't bend their arms and legs anymore. When that occurred, they were totally dependent on the other women to feed them, dress them, and help them with all other needs. The lucky ones often died not long after they had reached that stage of starvation. Their lives had become too miserable, their bodies too worn out.

As the war continued, the Japanese supplied us with less and less food. Even so, we were told that we should feel very privileged as we were "guests" of the Japanese emperor. Finally, we were told that we had to grow our own food using any seeds we could find or trade with people outside the camp. I guess our "welcome mat" had worn out.

Naturally, I didn't thrive very well under such harsh conditions with so little food. And, being exposed to so many diseases, I was sick almost constantly. At ten months I weighed a mere eight pounds — a common birth weight for newborns.

When I was about 18 months old, I had to have a small, non-cancerous tumor taken off my back because it opened frequently when I lay on my back and bled heavily. Because the chance of infection was so high and the Japanese guards were in a good mood, an operation in the hospital was allowed. Even though the surgery was done in the hospital outside the camp, it was performed under very bad, unsanitary conditions. The surgery took place early in the day, and we were sent back to the camp almost immediately after the operation was finished.

As soon as we returned, the nurse checked me over. She shook her head with worry; it didn't take her long to see how bad off I was. She informed my mother that my chance of surviving that operation was very slim, but that my chances of staying alive would be fairly good if I made it through the night. In the few hours since the surgery an infection had already set in. No medications, not even an aspirin, were given even though I already had a very high fever.

Miraculously, I managed to stay alive without any aspirin or other treatment. The infection left me with a large scar on my back as a remembrance of that operation. The scar is so big that I have to explain how I got it whenever a new physician examines me. They all wonder if I was ever operated on my lung. Under normal conditions that scar would be hardly visible after a couple of years.

While I was in surgery my mother was approached by a Catholic nun and asked to smuggle some bacon back into the camp and to give it to the other nuns there. My mother did not really want to do it because she knew how dangerous that was. Severe punishment would follow if the Japanese found out about it. But she did take the chance, hoping and praying that she would get a few small pieces for us. She knew how much we would enjoy it and would help us emotionally and physically. Anything different and better, such as a few morsels of bacon, was something that everyone would remember for a long time and would keep them going for quite a while.

When my mom arrived back in the camp, she gave the bacon to the nun who was very happy to receive it. She asked the nun if she could keep a little piece of it, not for herself, but to help my brother and me. She explained my condition to her, and how much I needed something to eat that was more nutritional than what I had been given so far. The nun replied that she was terribly sorry but she just knew that Mother Superior wouldn't want her to do that. I sometimes wonder if Mother Superior really knew about it or if the nun wanted to keep it all for herself.

My mother was deeply hurt by that gesture, and subsequently her faith in the Catholic Church and its beliefs were shattered forever. She wondered how someone could be so insensitive to the need of another human being, especially when they had risked so much for their gain. How could someone be so uncaring after having vowed to help other people in need? I like to believe that Mother Superior didn't know about my mother's request for a bit of bacon for a desperately sick child. However, my experiences with the nuns were not much better while I was growing up, and subsequently I also lost all respect for the Catholic Church.

The conditions in all the camps were terrible. As I said before, we were repeatedly told that we were "guests of the Emperor," and we should feel very much honored. Everything that needed to be done in the camp including maintenance, was handled by the "guests." This wasn't so bad when the necessary materials were available. After all, it was nice to have something to do, and it made the day go by faster. It also gave one something to concentrate on other than the conditions in the camp. But doing the repairs without the necessary materials later became intolerable. Initially the women became very innovated when badly needed materials weren't available. They learned how to use things creatively, making things work somehow, but as the war lasted longer it became harder and harder to find materials to fix things. The women also had to be very clever; even to figure out how to make their own toothbrushes since the war dragged on, and the old toothbrushes wore out.

All the chores in the camps were divided up by a camp leader chosen by the women in the camp. The women either volunteered for different duties or they were assigned to them. The jobs ranged from cooking meals to standing in big barrels of human manure and emptying out these barrels by hand or with a shell from a coconut. There were no toilets. The women who did the latter chores were exposed to many types of bacteria, making them even more susceptible to different diseases. Whenever antiseptic solutions were available, they were able to scrub down as soon as their chores were finished. My mother often volunteered for that particular job because she would be rewarded with a little extra food. People who did the more taxing or less desirable chores received slightly more food.

Preparing meals might sound like an easy job, but cooking something with hardly any ingredients and making it taste halfway palatable was difficult. The cooks had to stand over an open fire for hours, usually in the heat of the day, and make choices of what to cook with the little bit of ingredients they had, while simultaneously figuring out what to do with the bugs that were in the food. When it was time to dish out the food to the inhabitants of the camp, they often got a lot of complaints. Why couldn't they make something better, something tastier? Couldn't they cook more food? Having something to eat was the only thing people looked forward to, and when it looked and tasted like garbage, tempers rose. Of course, when told that they could gladly have the job, no one volunteered.

The water barrels that everyone got their drinking water from had a thick layer of bugs on the bottom of the barrel and other bugs were floating on top. They didn't have the time or energy to empty the barrels, clean them out, and fill them with clean water. However, that wouldn't have made much difference as they soon would be in the same condition again. They didn't tell anyone, and everyone drank bug-filled, contaminated water.

There was a lot of turmoil in the camp for several reasons. First of all, the women had to get used to living in conditions so opposite of what they were accustomed to. Most of them, like my mom, had lived a life of luxury and ease. They had to get used to not only living in very small, cramped living areas but to having absolutely no privacy at all. While trying to go to sleep, they had to become accustomed to hearing people moan and groan and cry. They had to share soap, combs and brushes, and even personal things like toothbrushes with each other.

They had to endure not knowing what was going on outside the camp, what was happening to their boyfriends, husbands, and sons. Were they being tortured? Were they still alive? Were they sick? They wondered how long the war was going to last. The Japanese didn't share any news about what was going on in the rest of the world. They wondered if anybody knew that they were being kept against their will.

There also was a lot of turmoil because they never knew what to expect. The punishments for not living by the rules were severe, often unexpected, and definitely not fitting. The rules were set up by the camp commanders and how strictly they were enforced depended on the commander and the mood he was in at the time of the rule infraction.

If one woman in the camp did something that displeased the Japanese, the whole camp could be, and usually was, punished. One form of punishment consisted of forcing everyone to stand straight and tall outside during the hottest hours of the day. Any cover on the head, such as a hat or a scarf, was not allowed. If the Japanese didn't think you were standing straight enough, they would take a stick and beat you in the back to force you to stand straighter. Nobody was allowed to make a sound or fall down, even though they were weak from heat exhaustion or malnutrition. Even babies weren't allowed to make any sound. If they cried or whimpered, the mother was told to make sure the noise stopped. It did not matter if the baby was very young, exhausted, or sick. If the commander was in a "good" mood he might tolerate some poor posture or whimpering. That didn't happen very often though.

Sometimes a woman's punishment was to kneel for hours on graveled ground under the hot tropical sun, or with the rain pouring down on her. No food or water was given during the punishment. To make sure that her knees were kept in the gravel and that she wouldn't lean back on her heels, the Japanese would put a metal bar on the back of her legs. The bar was covered with barbed wire and if she fell back on it because she was too weak to hold herself up, she would do great harm to her legs and buttocks. You could hear her screaming all over the camp. The person kneeling was not allowed to get up during the punishment time, not even if she had to use the toilet. Other punishments were severe beatings, isolation without food or water, or even death in a variety of ways.

Trading with people outside the camp was extremely dangerous as it was not allowed. It was done whenever possible though as the outsiders had things like medication, milk, food, cigarettes, or whatever the prisoners were asking for. If the Japanese found out, the violator was punished immediately and everyone including the children had to watch them being punished. The sentence for trading through the fence was often the death sentence, especially later in the war. How the execution was conducted depended on the preference of the camp commander.

Methods ranged from stabbing the prisoner to death with whatever was handy at the time to strapping the prisoner to a pole in the middle of the camp and leaving her there until she was dead. When the pole method was used, no one was allowed to come close enough to the victim to do anything for her. The prisoners were forced to look at her from time to time and listen to her suffering. The rest of the camp was always forced to watch the condemned woman's torture to remind them of the consequences of doing anything that was not permitted. This was supposed to teach us a lesson about what would happen if we were "bad."

In some camps a woman could be set on fire for something as innocent as trading through the fence. Maybe a baby needed some extra food, or someone needed quinine for malaria and could be saved by such a trade. Some mothers would do whatever it took to save their baby even if it meant that they could die themselves. Sometimes, a woman was strapped against a pole and sweet, syrupy liquid was poured all over her. In no time at all, she was covered with biting ants and itching all over the place. She couldn't scratch as her hands were tied behind her back. All the punishments were horrible but didn't stop the people from trading as they all hoped they could get away with it.

Between the time I was two and three our camp was severely punished. We received no food whatsoever for three days. One boy died because of his already weakened condition and the additional strain on his body because of the lack of food. He was three months older than I and he had started out life in better health than I, but he died, and I lived through it. I have often wondered why I stayed alive, and he didn't.

Some camp commanders were more humane than others were. If that was the case, a weakened or sick baby would be cared for by women who were too sick to stand in the sun. They weren't in very good shape themselves or they would have been ordered to stand in the hot sun as well. Caring for a sick infant was not an easy task for someone who was sick herself, but everyone tried to help others as much as they could. Sometimes that was nearly impossible, because everyone became weaker and weaker as the war progressed.

If anyone disobeyed orders, or did not live strictly by the rules, the duration of the punishments was increased. If an infraction of the rules occurred and the Japanese didn't know who had done it, the whole camp had to stand in line in the sun until the guilty woman confessed. When that happened, the guilty woman was punished in front of the others or tortured behind closed doors so badly that her screams were unbearable even when heard from a distance. When she rejoined the other women, they would often yell at her because they themselves wouldn't have been punished if she had obeyed the rules — or if she had admitted to her "crime" without delay.

When a child did something wrong, he or she was immediately punished by the mother. It was very important that the children didn't get into trouble. If the Japanese discovered that a child had done something wrong, the mother was sometimes punished for the child's behavior. Children were the full responsibility of the mothers even though they often weren't present when the children misbehaved. All the women capable of doing labor during the day weren't with their children. Regardless of the situation, the mothers were always accountable for the behavior of their children.

Sometimes the children were punished by the Japanese, which was doubly hard for the mother. She had to stand and listen helplessly as her child was beaten and screaming for help.

One time, towards the end of the war, my mother was put in the camp prison for six weeks for allegedly stealing some wood to build a fire. Each day she needed to find a way to boil water to cook my food in, or for me to drink. She didn't want to give me the bug-infested water. The Japanese didn't supply wood for fires to boil water for drinking, so my mother had to find wood herself.

One day my mother was caught picking up a wooden box that supposedly belonged to the Japanese. She knew that it didn't belong to them because she would never have picked it up if there was the slightest doubt about who it belonged to. At that point during the war, she wouldn't have risked being punished by them and not be able to care for her children. We had been in the camps well over two years and she didn't have the energy to endure any unnecessary hardship. The guard decided that it was his box and that she had stolen from the Japanese emperor.

To this day, Mother hasn't told us much about what happened in the prison during those six weeks. The only thing I know is that the prison room was filled way beyond capacity, and the women could relieve themselves only whenever the guards decided to let them go to the bathroom. This meant they had to wait way past the time they actually needed to go. Since she couldn't wait that long, she drank very little and became even more dehydrated. Her six-week ordeal must have been very, very painful, too painful for her to talk about. She not only endured her punishment but also at the same time was terribly worried about what was happening to my brother and me.

While Mother was in the camp prison other women had to take care of my brother and me. We were a tremendous burden since everyone already had plenty of things to do and worry about, let alone take on the care of someone else's children. I was sick most of the time and coughed endlessly because of my chronic bronchitis. I was about two and a half years old at that time. My mother suspected that the woman whom she trusted, because she was a close friend and was supposed to be the main caretaker of us, tried to choke me to death while I was in her care.

I sometimes get flashbacks of being choked by someone, and to this day I feel like I'm being suffocated when I get hot or when the temperature around me is hot and muggy like the tropics. She later found out that this woman put my brother and me outside on the veranda at night, instead of keeping us close by to watch us. She didn't want to listen to us crying or me coughing.

When my mother was finally released from the prison camp, she soon discovered that this woman had also taken all the sugar she had saved for me and hidden so carefully. That sugar was desperately needed to feed me, keep me alive, and help me keep my strength whenever my mother couldn't get anything else that I could tolerate. But she was happy to be united with us again and to be alive.

The terror in the camps was often so extreme that solidarity was often impossible. One never knew what was going to happen next and what was considered permissible one day was not necessarily okay the next. There was no logic behind the use and abuse of rules, nor was there any way to know what kind of punishment was going to be meted out for the supposed breaking of rules. Many survivors of the Japanese camps have stated that the moods of many Japanese commanders depended on the phases of the moon. The Japanese would become even more unpredictable when there was a full moon.

We were told over and over that we were only fourth-class citizens. The Japanese were the "superior" race, far more superior to anyone else on this earth. The Japanese men were first class citizens followed in rank by Japanese women. Men of other races were third class, and their women came last, in the final position of fourth-class.

We were regarded as human "dogs." The small amounts of food they so "graciously" brought into the camp for us was often thrown onto the ground, and sometimes even driven over by their trucks before we were allowed to pick it up. Nothing was wrapped in those days, and things like sugar and flour were also just thrown on the ground.

Some women became very resourceful at finding and keeping seeds to grow new crops. They also became very imaginative at making things from scraps or anything else they could find. Items like toothbrushes and soap were not supplied and were either shared or made from whatever people could find.

The Japanese seemed to get pleasure out of seeing us suffer, but admitted after the war that they had initially believed their job of keeping a bunch of women under control would be easy. The Japanese women were always very submissive and would do whatever their husbands, or any man, told them to do. They soon found out that we weren't like that at all. The Japanese officers couldn't seem to put us down permanently. They confessed that although they had tried to break us mentally, we always seemed to be able to recover no matter how weak we were. We preferred death to totally submitting to them.

Another obstacle we all encountered was the fact that we did not understand the language or the customs of our captors. The Japanese didn't know our language or our customs but were not concerned about that as we were their captives. They sometimes spoke to us in broken English, and most of the women had enough English knowledge to understand them. The ones who didn't understand English were told by others what was happening. Occasionally, there would be a woman in the camp who understood some Japanese and others slowly learned the language, probably as a survival method to find out what was going on. She wouldn't let on that she knew what was being said by the Japanese guards but quietly would tell others.

We soon learned that the Japanese didn't want us to look them in the eyes because this behavior showed disrespect. We always had to bow whenever we saw a Japanese soldier, making sure that we looked down to the ground while backing away from him. When we had to stand for a head count, or when we had to stand in the hot sun for punishment, we had to make sure that our heads were bowed, and we looked down when they came around to check on us.

From birth on, I was surrounded by hate for the Japanese, hate for the living conditions, and hate for some fellow prisoners who made our lives miserable by complaining or who endangered our lives by their behavior. However, I was also surrounded by love — not only that of my mother and brother, but also of other women in the camp. They showed their love for children and for their fellow prisoners as well. This could be seen in the way they took care of each other and in the things, they would do or give up to help each other.

Things didn't go well all the time though, especially as years passed and food and items to trade became less available. There were days when the women fought amongst each other over whatever they had to trade, such as jewelry, coffee, or cigarettes, for duties or a couple of extra crumbs of food. But when someone really needed something almost everyone tried to help as much as possible.

I was also surrounded by people who were survivors, who refused to give up. They struggled to stay alive against all odds or to make other women's lives as comfortable as possible. The true inner strength of each interned woman became apparent and sometimes surprised other prisoners.

Death was not new to me as it came more and more often, to mothers as well as to children, as the war continued. Sometimes mothers gave some of their food to their children, in the belief that it helped them. The mothers were told repeatedly that they needed to eat their portion themselves to survive and take care of their children. But for some mothers it was too painful to hear their hungry children cry and beg for more food, as they grew thinner and weaker. The mothers would cave in and give up some of their own rations. This caused them to become weaker and some of them died, leaving their children behind to be taken care of by whoever volunteered to do so. After the war, those children were brought to family members, if they could be found, or placed in orphanages.

When someone in the camp died, the women that had enough strength to take on the burden of digging a grave had to carry the dead body to it also. The Japanese didn't do that chore. The women had to make a simple wooden box coffin themselves. When the women became weaker and could not make coffins themselves, or weren't able to dig graves, the Japanese sometimes assisted. If they helped with making a coffin for the burial or digging the hole to put the coffin in, they made it whatever size they wanted to, usually the size that would fit a Japanese woman — much smaller than most Western prisoners. If the coffin was too small, and it was the only one available, the body still had to fit inside somehow.

Bodies had to be buried fast because of the climate. The women in charge of burying the body had to bend the legs or arms and do whatever was necessary to make the body fit into the coffin. This was an especially painful task. Not only were there many sentimental feelings about burying a friend or family member, but often the body was in such a condition that there was a lot of build-ups of fluids that made it extremely hard to bend the arms or legs. I was spared the actual sight of all of this, but I heard in detail about it since there was no privacy and everyone knew everything that happened in the camps.

Initially, the older children were able to play with each other and with the toys that had been brought into the camps. For a while, their lives were still somewhat normal. They didn't always realize what they were up against and what was in their future. They were fenced in, but they had different outlets that allowed them to tolerate what was happening. They could become involved in their games long enough to forget what was happening around them.

In the beginning of the war, they were allowed to go to classes for short periods of time during the day when the teachers had some time off. The classes were usually taught by the nuns in the camp or by a schoolteacher if there was one in the camp. They practiced songs, memorized children's poems, and learned whatever children learn in the early years of school. Little by little as the war progressed, all the toys were broken or destroyed, and the prisoners' resourcefulness led to the use of whatever was available to make simple toys. Imaginary games were played as well as games that did not require any toys, such as hide and seek.

The Japanese soon forbade the teaching of classes of any kind and any instruction had to take place in secret. Books and writing materials had to be hidden, especially anything that resembled a diary. The punishments were extremely severe if the Japanese found them. They didn't think it was necessary for the children to learn new things and for the women to take time to teach them. They definitely didn't want anybody to write down what had been happening to them during their internment.

The children's lives became more and more bleak. Finally, their energy levels became so low that they couldn't concentrate long enough to learn anything, or they simply didn't care anymore. Their teachers weren't much better off, and it was getting harder and harder to find new supplies such as paper, pencils, or textbooks. The children just sat around and waited for their next meals or for some attention from their mothers or others.

The babies were fairly isolated for most of the day. Babies and children who needed more care than just meals and diaper changes were cared for by the women who were either too old or too sick to do any of the real chores. This often meant that they were left unattended and didn't get the emotional support or the physical care they needed so much, especially so early in life.

As a newborn I was kept in a basket about the size of a large picnic basket with a very thin mattress in it. Every morning my mother had to take me and the basket outside and clean the lice and other insects out of the basket, and off me before putting me back in my basket again, only to have it fill up very quickly during the day.

After a couple of years my basket was either too small for me or the heat had rotted it away. Anyway, my mother had saved up some coffee and found someone who was willing to trade it for a used playpen. This enabled me to see a little bit more of what was going on around me. However, I still wasn't getting much stimulation like children get with toys they can play with and learn from. I mainly saw the roof and the walls of the room we were in.

My mother had a terrible time keeping me comfortable because the housing provided by the Japanese was such that it was very hard to keep any of us dry. The roofs often leaked and the only time they were fixed was when the women put whatever they could find on them to slow down the rain. Those sleeping in the top bunks would get wet from the rain, but those on a lower bunk often didn't fare much better. They also might get wet, but not from the rain. They might get wet from the women sleeping above who were either too weak or apathetic to climb down and walk to the latrine at night. Others were in such deteriorating physical states that they couldn't maintain bladder control at all, so they wet the bed. Whether from rain or urine, one often got wet, and it is debatable as to who got the better deal, the ones who slept in the top bunk or the ones who slept below. The stench must have been terrible no matter where you slept.

When I was about two and a half years old, we were put in yet another camp, near Aek Pamienke, the third one to which we were assigned. The trip to that camp was horrendous and many of the people who made the trip as children old enough to remember that day still suffer from post-traumatic stress syndrome or other severe problems.

Everyone had to get up early in the morning and get their few belongings ready and packed. Then they had to walk to the train station where the horrible train ride began. The windows of the train had been blackened and locked tightly, making it impossible to see where we were going or to open them so we would get some fresh air. The train was filled way over capacity. The seats had been taken out and we were forced to sit or stand on the floors of the cars. We were transported like cattle being brought to the slaughterhouse. It was a very long, slow, ride that lasted about 10 hours. We didn't travel a great distance, just deeper into the jungle, farther away from civilization.

The smell of being cramped in small quarters with no ventilation was repulsive. Locked up with no fresh air and inside temperatures that kept climbing higher and higher, some of us become claustrophobic and very uncomfortable. Could my breathing problems triggered by heat have something to do with this? I often wonder. There were no toilets on the trains, so everyone at some time during the trip had to urinate. The thin pieces of clothing we were wearing hardly kept the urine from going onto the floor. With no ventilation the stench soon became very unbearable.

No food or water was supplied during the journey. When the train finally stopped, everyone was ordered to get off and to walk the rest of the journey in the hot sun, approximately five miles. Since this was three years after the original imprisonment, none of the women or children had much energy left to walk that far. Everyone also had to carry whatever belongings they still had plus help the young children and, if necessary, carry them.

At this point, my mother was no longer capable of carrying me for any distance, even though I was at the age that I should have been able to walk. I couldn't even crawl yet. My mother sat down at the side of the road with me in her arms, and my brother next to her on one side, and her few belongings on the other side. Sitting down was a very dangerous thing to do because the Japanese did not tolerate this for any reason. She couldn't help it as she just didn't have any energy left.

Fortunately for all of us, she received unexpected help. Jeeps from the train station to the camp transported the very sick people. One person on a jeep passing by grabbed me from my mother and yelled, "You will get her back in the camp." This helped my mother somewhat, but she now had to worry if and when she would find me again. The camps were all very big and she had no idea who had taken me out of her arms. It had all happened too fast. She and my brother managed to walk to the camp, and she was able to find me soon after arriving in the camp. Fortunately, I don't remember any of this.

When my mother and my brother reached the camp, they didn't have all our belongings with them. It wasn't that we had that much left, but they both had barely enough strength and energy to walk, much less carry things with them. They had to leave behind the playpen I slept in because it was just too heavy and big. The next day my mother returned to the train depot to pick up the playpen, walking the ten-mile roundtrip in one day and again leaving me behind. At least I had my brother with me part of the day this time. I'm sure he didn't spend every minute with me, but I must have known that he was not too far away.

My mother always volunteered for extra work so that she could get extra food to share with us. The extra food wasn't a large amount, but anything was better than nothing. It also meant that she was not around much for me or my brother. I was often left behind in the care of whomever would or could take care of me. When she came back from working hard, she was exhausted and didn't have much energy left to spend time with us. There wasn't a lot of time for bonding and nurturing, or for building the trust that comes from knowing that someone is always there for you.

My brother, who was almost five when the war started, was initially in much better shape than I was, both mentally and physically. He had received very good nutrition for his first five years and had been rather chubby. This was good as he had some reserve to carry him through the war. He also had proper child development care during those years, and had been exposed to colors, toys, dexterity problems, puzzles, etc.; all the things that help children develop better. Although he lost out on a lot of living and developing while in the camps, he seems to have fared better than many in the camps who were about the same age as he. He claims not to remember anything about those three and a half years.

Although the Japanese officers treated the women very badly, the little children were often treated a little more gently. Maybe the guards were thinking about their own children they had left behind or maybe they wanted to befriend the "guests" through their children. Some survivors have said that they saw the Japanese give children a piece of fruit or candy. My mother later told us that my brother was given cigarettes by the Japanese and that he started smoking as early as six or seven years of age. They would give cigarettes to any child who wanted them. Whether or not the Japanese tried to win over the women through the children will never be known for sure. However, if that was their objective, they didn't succeed. As for my brother, he had to go through cigarette withdrawal at the ripe old age of eight when the war ended. My mother told me that she even tried to help him to quit smoking by telling him he wouldn't get any chicken if he still smoked, when the chicken was fat and big enough to be slaughtered. I believe this was after the war was over. Somehow, she had got a hold of a scrawny chicken which she gave extra rations of food to fatten it up. She kept it tied with a string to a post. We all looked forward to getting some real meat for a change. When we finally got to eat the chicken, my brother didn't get any as he was still smoking occasionally. However, according to him, he didn't get any chicken because my mother had seen him stick his tongue out at me. I don't remember anything about it so I really don't know why he didn't get the chicken.

My brother was very lucky that he was of normal size and appearance once he lost all his extra weight. He could have easily looked older than his age according to Japanese standards. My mom never had to worry whether he would be taken away and send to the men's camps. The Japanese figured that a boy of a certain size (whatever that was in their minds) was big enough to do hard work since most of the European twelve-year-old boys were close to the size of adult Japanese men. The transfer of the boys from the women's camp to a men's camp was always done without much warning and mothers were never told too far ahead of time when this would happen. On the day that the boy(s) would be going to another camp the Japanese would tell the mothers whose sons would be moved, and that they had to have them ready at a certain time later that same day, usually just a couple of hours later. The move would have been a good opportunity to give a boy a note to pass on to a husband of a woman in the camp. However, no notes were sent along, and little information was passed from one camp to the next since no one knew who the boy was going to see in his new camp and the mothers didn't want to endanger the lives of their children. Boys occasionally ended up in the same camp as their father, but this was never known ahead of time since the Japanese did not want any messages to be passed on from one camp to the other.

With such short notice the mothers had to have the few belongings all packed up with barely enough time to say goodbye. This was always an extremely sad event not only for mothers who had just lost their boys, but for the boys themselves as well. Their departure had a tremendous impact on most of the members in the camp. Everyone knew that the conditions for the boys would be a lot worse than they had known so far. They would be expected to perform hard labor instead of light duties or playing. Also, not knowing where their young children were going and what exactly they were going to endure was sometimes too hard to bear for the women, especially in the case of an only child. My mother was fortunate that she didn't have to worry about her only son being taken away.

When the war was over, I was almost three years old, and was just learning to walk with the help of two women holding me up. I still couldn't stand up by myself and was still extremely weak and sick because of malnutrition along with high fevers, bronchitis, pneumonia and other diseases. I also didn't have much opportunity to crawl or exercise to make my legs and body stronger, as I had been kept in a basket or a playpen with not much to look at but walls and bunks. If the weather was right and the women had the time and energy to carry me outside, I could see the sky. This did not happen too often; certainly not after the war had been going on for a while.

Under normal conditions babies develop more during the first two years of their life than at any other time except in the womb. Physical skills such as reaching for objects, sitting up, crawling and walking depend on the development of the muscles, the nervous system, and other body systems which depend on nourishment the body receives and exercising the muscles. I had a lot of catching up to do later because of deprivation early in life and this proved to be a long and very slow process.

On August 15, 1945, the war finally ended. Yet we weren't allowed to express our happiness when we found out that we were free or be assured that things would be better from now on. Initially the Japanese officers denied the rapidly growing rumors of impending peace and the guards believed them. They kept thinking that they were invincible. As long as the officers said the war was not over, it was not over.

Finally, pamphlets with news of the end of the war started falling from the sky. The instructions were very specific, and we were told to keep quiet as the Allied Forces feared — rightfully so — that the Japanese would be angered by any show of emotion. If somebody cheered, looked the Japanese guards in the eyes, or did something that upset them, they would kill that person. Their disappointment of having lost the war was that great. A few women who had survived more than three years of living hell needlessly died because they couldn't contain their happiness and did something that made the guards so furious that they lost their tempers and killed them. The Japanese were very upset that they, the super race, had lost the war. All the joy of finally being freed, of not having to worry about starvation and other punishments, of being able to bathe, have your own toothbrush and bar of soap, of finally being able to eat real food and drink uncontaminated water and the knowledge that life would change for the better had to be kept silent and inside oneself.

Initially the situation in the camps didn't change a lot other than that the rules weren't enforced anymore, and there seemed to be a bit more food available to us. We were also finally given medication when necessary. But, for many it was too late.

Right before the war ended my mother had developed beriberi (a thiamine deficiency disease), a high fever, and a severe case of erysipelas, an acute infectious disease caused by streptococcus which results in fevers and chills and a rapidly spreading deep-red inflammation of the skin. When the war was over and her condition had still not changed, she was allowed to go to the hospital for care, as it was feared that she might get blood poisoning. While she was in the hospital for a couple of weeks, my brother and I were put in the care of the Salvation Army. They did a wonderful job taking care of us and feeding us, but it was still another time of separation from my mother, a total of three times in the first three years of my life.

Once the Japanese acknowledged that the war had really ended, they had to admit it to us. This was an extremely hard undertaking for them. After all, weren't they the super race? Now they had to reunite the surviving family members, also not an easy matter. The men came from camps all over the islands and as far away as Burma and India. Arrangements also had to be made with the Dutch authorities for transportation back to the Netherlands. All these matters took time.

As soon as we were liberated, the Indonesian people declared their desire for independence. They wanted all ties with the Dutch broken and ordered us to go back to the Netherlands as soon as possible. This was much unexpected and therefore could not be done immediately as there were a lot of plans to be made. The Indonesians became more and more hostile towards us. We now needed protection from them and the only ones available to do that were the Japanese. Suddenly we had to trust and rely on the very same people who had treated us so badly before. What a horrible and confusing experience it must have been for someone as small as I was at the time. Later British and American soldiers came to protect us and they did a great job taking care of us.

I was told that the end of the war came not a moment too soon. The Japanese had plans and drawings of gas chambers similar to the ones the Germans had used, and they were ready to start construction. One can assume who would be building these gas chambers — the prisoners who built the railroad tracks in the jungles for them so they could send their supplies in and out faster. If the war had lasted any longer, I might not have been around to write this book.

One might assume that survivors of the camps would be grateful and happy to be alive. Most of them were. However, many of them still live in turmoil questioning why they survived the camps while others did not. Some have a sense of guilt about not having done more for their friends and are wondering what they could have done differently.

After I learned about what had happened to me the first three years of my life, I often wonder why I stayed alive while others did not. I know that I couldn't have helped anybody survive. I was simply too young to be of any help to anyone. I have never felt guilty about being alive, just very curious. I also wonder why I, having been in such a poor condition, stayed alive while others who seemingly were in better health did not survive the war.

Some survivors suffered from post-traumatic stress syndrome (PTSS) soon after the war was over. They had a horrible time adjusting to their new situation. But psychologists and other health care professionals didn't know much about the disorder until many years later so they couldn't help them with all the feelings and turmoil bottled up inside of them. Other people appeared to live normal lives for twenty or thirty years and then, suddenly, started having problems coping with life in general. Some complained of nightmares or of flashbacks of life in the camp. Other women didn't show serious problems until they reached menopause. PTSS has shown to affect people differently, and manifests as everything from specific phobias to a total inability to function in a normal world.

CHAPTER 3

It took us quite a while to be reunited with my dad because the authorities first had to find out where he was and then arrange for his return. They finally found out that he was in Burma, quite a distance from Sumatra. My mom had hoped that the four of us would be together before Christmas but that was not to be. Our reunion finally happened right before New Year's Eve of 1945. I can imagine how happy my parents were when they found out that all of us had survived the war. But what a sorry sight they must have been for each other.

My dad, who had weighed well over 300 pounds before the war, was less than half that weight, not much for a man who was at least six feet tall and of medium bone structure. My mom, who was over 200 pounds before the war, now weighed a scant 100 pounds. It was fortunate that they were both so heavy before the war started. At least they had reserves to draw on to survive.

After our parents were reunited, my brother and my dad got reacquainted first. What a happy reunion that was for both. Finally, it was time for my dad to be introduced to me, his daughter who had been given his first name, a tradition in those days. The eldest daughter was named after her father or his family while the eldest son was named after the mother or her family. According to my mom, my dad was not thrilled at all when he saw me and refused to believe that I was his daughter. He hadn't known about me until then because any messages my mother had sent to him were never received. People in the camps were allowed to send messages to their loved ones but they had to choose from prewritten sentences. Nothing else was allowed to be in the messages.

What a pitiful first impression I made. I looked just like those children from Bangladesh or third world countries that you see on television with little skinny, stick-like arms and legs, big bellies, and sunken, hollow cheeks. I could barely walk and was sick all the time. He simply didn't want to believe that such a sick and ugly child could be his own flesh and blood. In my weakened state I didn't look anything at all like him or my mother. He refused to accept that I was his child and treated me accordingly. To this day I don't know who he thought my real father might have been. I certainly don't look Japanese and there were never any white men in the women's camp nor was there any occasion for my mom to have been with another man. Besides that, my birth certificate states that I was born in September, a little more than six months after my parents were separated from each other.

The problem was that my parents had friends whose baby was born in May of 1942, just about four months before I was born. When the war was over, their baby didn't look anything at all like me. She was thin, but not extremely so, and overall, she looked much healthier than I did. She could walk and run, but I could barely walk by the time my father saw me. The reason she was in so much better shape than I was because she was much luckier from the start and had had several advantages over me. First, she wasn't born prematurely, and she was born earlier in the war which gave her mother time to give her proper nourishment that much longer. Also, she wasn't born in the concentration camp. Her parents didn't have to go to the camps right away because of the kind of job and position her dad held. For about one year they lived under prewar conditions where she had all the food and care she needed. When she and her mom finally did go to the camp, her mom was also able to smuggle in a nice supply of things like aspirin and other medications that helped her whenever she was sick.

So, when my parents were reunited and my father saw and compared me to that other baby he just couldn't imagine, and refused to believe, that I was his child. I suppose that he had gone through so much hell during the previous three and a half years that he couldn't deal with having to put up with something else that was not only a problem, but which reminded him continuously of what the war had done to his family. Now I was presented to him as his responsibility and something he had to make right.

To this day I vividly remember the day he finally recognized me as his child. Up until I was about twelve years old, I remained quite skinny. I had long hair, which was held back, tightly, in a thick ponytail. Even though I was proud of my ponytail most of the time, I longed to have my hair short, to have it like some of the other children in my class. Having it short, though, meant having to make regular trips to the beauty shop to keep it looking nice. The money spent on haircuts was needed to pay all the other bills we had. I really became tired of my long hair, though, and begged to have it cut short. Finally, I was allowed to do so.

Once my hair was cut and washed it fell loosely around my face. I looked like a totally different person. My dad had wavy, curly hair and when my hair was cut it had waves in it also. He took one look at me and said to my aunt, who was standing nearby, "She does look like one of us." I had never really known that my dad had not accepted me as his child, so I was very confused by his remark. I didn't know what he meant, and I didn't ask, because I was too confused by what had just happened. His words must have made a big impression on me because I still remember this event, even after all these years. I didn't learn until much later why he had behaved the way he had. I really don't know if it made such a difference in my life, knowing that I was indeed the daughter of this man who had the same last name as I. It certainly didn't feel different.

Since my parents knew they couldn't stay in Indonesia, the land they loved so much, they had to get used to the idea of starting over in the Netherlands. They could come back after a couple of years, if they desired to do so but they knew that they most likely wouldn't want to as the Indonesian people had already shown that they wouldn't be very welcome at all. Anyway, my parents hadn't been in the Netherlands since before the war and were wondering what they would be coming back to and what life would be like there now. Soon enough they would make the long trip back to their homeland and find out.

When the ships finally began to transport people back to the Netherlands, the weakest people and those in the worst physical condition were the first ones selected to go back. Because of my condition, we were on the first list for the people on the island of Sumatra. The boat was named the Noordam, which was at that time a freighter with limited accommodations for passengers. To be able to get more people on the boat, it had been transformed into a transport boat for troops. Much later it became a cruise ship.

Before we were allowed on board, the adults had to sign a paper saying that their children had already had the measles. The reason for this was the bad experience encountered by passengers on a boat that left the island of Java before our departure. During the trip back to the Netherlands there was an outbreak of measles among the children. Because of their weakened state and the conditions onboard the ship, many children developed pneumonia right after they contracted the measles. This was too much for their frail bodies and many of them died. They had survived three years of hell only to die before they were able to enjoy life again.

The doctors didn't want this to happen on later departures and therefore required the signing of the document. Most mothers lied about whether their children had had the measles or not. They told the doctors that their children had contracted the measles while in the camp. Whether the doctors believed this or not remains a mystery. Nevertheless, they allowed families to sail and probably assumed that the mothers weren't telling the truth. They certainly weren't going to tell the families that they had to stay behind. About a week or so before arrival in the Netherlands all the children were vaccinated for the measles. We never did understand why that was done but nobody asked. The serum they used was supposed to make the children have the measles. This assured that there wouldn't be a big outbreak of measles on board, and nobody would have any symptoms until they were back in the Netherlands.

The boat had cabins for 150 people but because of the circumstances it held 1,500 men, women, and children. During the day we had to stay on deck and at night we slept in hammocks which were hung across the whole room three rows high and four rows deep with a small path in between the rows.

Even though there was plenty of food aboard, most people couldn't eat much during the trip back. Their stomachs hadn't had much food for so long that they could only eat small portions at a time. Many people on board became seasick and couldn't eat. Dad proudly told us about all the food he could and would eat because there was so much left over. Because he had been a cook for the Japanese, he sometimes was able to eat larger amounts of food while in the camp, and sneak in a bite or two while preparing the meals. My mom was one of those people who couldn't eat very much. I didn't fare too well either. During our trip back, I came down with whooping cough. Sometimes I had a dozen coughing attacks per night and my mother had to go on deck and hold me up straight so I could keep on breathing. Even though I did receive some medication, it took a long time for me to get better. Miraculously I survived, but I sure didn't make it easy or enjoyable for my mom.

Finally, after six long weeks of traveling by boat past foreign countries, through the Suez Canal, the Mediterranean, and past Portugal, France and Belgium, we arrived in Rotterdam. Upon our arrival in Rotterdam, we were processed and put on a bus or train to our destination to meet with my grandparents. The small town they lived in, Haren, is near Groningen which is the capital of the province also named

Groningen. The Netherlands as a country is subdivided into provinces which might be compared to counties here in the United States. Just to give you an idea how large the Netherlands is, the entirety of the Netherlands fits into both Maricopa and Pinal County, Arizona.

My parents decided to move in with my grandparents because they had a large enough house to share with us. Despite its much colder climate, living conditions in Groningen bore some similarity to Sumatra. All the houses in that part of the Netherlands were rather large and there were sizeable yards (for Dutch standards) around them and much open country. It was a beautiful place to come back to and heal after all that we had been through during the previous four years. With the ample space in and around the house, it was an ideal location for children to play when the weather was warm enough, and it wasn't raining.

We had a long train ride to Haren as we had to change trains two or three times. My grandfather, who was a medical doctor, took one look at me and said he couldn't believe his eyes. In front of him was a girl three and a half years old but only the size and weight of a one-year-old. How could she possibly have survived like that, he wondered? Nonetheless, he and my grandmother were very happy to see us all. About five days after our arrival my brother and I got the measles. According to my mom I came down with it quite suddenly, almost from one minute to the next. She said that I was talking and laughing with my grandmother and suddenly became very ill. I followed up my bout with the measles with another severe case of pneumonia. My brother showed symptoms much more gradually and since he was in better shape, he was well in a relatively short time.

My grandfather thought it was best that I be admitted to the Academisch Ziekenhuis in Groningen, which is similar to a University Hospital here in the United States. He wanted me to have a thorough check-up since he was extremely concerned about my condition. Because I was so weak and small, I was put on a special diet to gain weight and was ordered to have lots of rest. I wasn't supposed to get overtired or worn out, something I would hear for many years to come. In the beginning, I received only one teaspoon of milk each hour and gradually got larger portions of milk and other foods. I probably wanted to have more than those small portions, but I was told that my stomach couldn't hold any more food than that.

I still have a problem with wanting to eat more than I need, and continue to want to catch up for lost time. During my hospital stay I had an extensive checkup. Because of all the coughing I did, I was x-rayed, and they found a couple of spots on my lungs. One was the size of a silver dollar. Then the doctor put me in quarantine for 48 hours because they were afraid that I had tuberculosis. Here again, I had another separation from my family. I am sure I didn't realize why this was necessary, and why my mom and dad couldn't see me again. I must have wondered if I would ever be able to stay with them permanently. After more tests and check-ups, it was decided that the spots on my lung were just scar tissue from all the coughing I had done throughout my first three years in the camp. My lungs were checked regularly by x-ray and the spots slowly disappeared completely by the time I was about 10 years old.

Even though my parents had both survived the camp and were able to go on with their lives, things were not like pre-war conditions. Apart from having to deal with regaining their own health, they also began a new life in a country where they soon found out they weren't welcome, and they couldn't speak openly about what had happened to them. The colonial Dutch who had just returned from hell on earth could not vent their feelings about any of their horrible experiences of the previous three and a half years.

They expected to be treated with respect and dignity. After all, they had come home to their own people and to their own country. They were Dutch citizens just like the European Dutch who had endured the war and should have had the same rights. Instead, their fellow countrymen resented them for coming back and for wanting housing and jobs. The Dutch who lived in the Netherlands during the war had gone through hell because of the Germans. They reasoned that the people coming from Indonesia had been much better off since they had been warm every day. One look at all of them with their tanned bodies made the homeland Dutch people look very pale and sickly.

They didn't realize that a person could be too warm, suffer from dehydration and sunburn, and be exposed to horrible diseases known only in the tropics. They were not interested in hearing about the hardships the Dutch colonials had encountered while living in Indonesia because they had just survived the coldest winter in history with not much to heat their homes and with a severe food shortage. Many Dutch people had to burn their furniture to get some heat, and eat tulip bulbs, rats, or whatever they could find. They were in a weakened condition as well and many didn't survive the last winter. After the war there was a severe housing shortage because the Germans had heavily bombed the Netherlands during the war. They were definitely not prepared to receive all the people who had been living in Indonesia.

Most of the people returning from Indonesia now had to live in cold, damp apartments with no central heat, no water heaters, and no bath or shower. Some of them, having been born in Indonesia and never have lived or traveled elsewhere, had not gone through winters like the ones in the Netherlands. They had never seen snow, sleet, and ice. This was a far cry from prewar conditions in Indonesia where one took baths sometimes three times a day and where homes had been spacious, comfortable, and the climate warm. They just didn't like living like that. This caused a lot of anger and bitterness not only in my parents but in most of the survivors.

These pent-up emotions were naturally reflected in the relationship my parents had with us and with each other and they turned their anger toward anyone who was not 100 percent white. I felt a lot of resentment while I was growing up because of all this anger. For a long time, I did not understand where the anger came from or why I had so much in me and why there was so much anger in them.

Nobody told me what we had endured, all the losses we had suffered, and all the cruel and inhumane conditions we had lived with and survived. Everything was just held inside. Much later I learned about what had happened and was able to slowly look at things differently. I was able to forgive my parents for the way they had treated us because now I understood where their feelings came from. I realized that they had done their best, but had been robbed overnight, not only of all their worldly possessions, but of their fantastic lifestyle as well, never to regain any of it. They had lived under the most horrendous conditions for well over three years, somehow surviving where many others, often close friends, did not. And finally, when the war was over, they had looked forward to starting a new life in Indonesia, which is where they wanted to stay, but couldn't since it was unsafe because of unrest among the Indonesian people.

CHAPTER 4

I was three and a half years old, and my brother was almost nine when we started our recuperation. I was at the age where children in the Netherlands attend kindergarten three hours in the morning and two hours in the afternoon with a two-hour break for lunch. Yet I was not allowed to go to school since I was too weak and needed to gain weight and strength. Since I had just started to walk going to school would have been too taxing for me.

Finally, at age five I was allowed to go to kindergarten, but only in the mornings as it was believed (I don't know by whom) that I needed to rest in the afternoon. Even though I don't remember anything about my kindergarten days, I feel that I must have been very happy to go to school. I'm sure I enjoyed the contact with the other kids and the freedom of not having someone watch every move I made.

Even though my dad was almost 49 years old on his arrival in the Netherlands, he soon got a job checking on companies and factories to ensure the right amount of food coupons were given out so that nobody received more than their allotment. How he got that job I don't know, as he didn't have any experience in that field. There was a scarcity of certain food items and necessities to make life more comfortable, so every family was given a designated amount of food coupons depending on the size of the family. The job involved traveling all over the province of Groningen, which was a very rural province, and the towns and cities were far apart.

This was not an easy job for my dad, as he had to take buses and trains to get from one place to another. How he must have missed his car! This mode of transportation was especially difficult in the winter because the bus stops were out in the open and very cold. Waiting for the train was a bit better because the covered train stations were usually somewhat warmer and at least he would be out of the rain, sleet or snow. Having to walk to the bus station and wait for the bus made the whole ordeal even worse. How cold he must have felt, and how he must have missed the nice warm sun in Indonesia. But he had no other choice as very few people owned a car, and the ones who did were the rich. I can really appreciate what he must have gone through. I now live in a warm climate, and certainly don't miss the cold winters, rain, snow and damp conditions where I previously lived. And I definitely wouldn't want to be without a car!

On rainy days my dad not only had to walk around with wet clothing but would have to sit in his wet clothes during his appointments and pretend he was comfortable and happy. One of his sisters, who lived in Den Haag, talked him into moving there. She had spare rooms in her apartment and was told by the authorities that she needed to rent those out because she had more room than needed to live there with her family. She really didn't have that much extra room, especially not compared with what most people have these days. But, with the housing shortage the way it was, every apartment had to have the maximum amount of people in it. If the housing authorities decided that you had too much empty space, they would tell you that you had to take in boarders. If you didn't know anyone, they would find you the appropriate number of people to live with you.

When they had told her that she needed to rent out part of her apartment she thought of my mom and dad. Naturally, she preferred to have her own family there rather than someone she didn't know at all. Besides solving the housing problem, she also felt that my father might have a better chance of finding more suitable work for himself on the west coast where the population was denser and more work available.

Den Haag (The Hague) is the capital of the province of Zuid-Holland as well as the seat of the Dutch government. Also, the International Court of Justice, "The Peace Palace," is located there. All those government buildings needed personnel to keep them going. My aunt knew that the chances of my dad finding a more suitable job in Den Haag would be much better for him. He didn't really have much choice, because by then there was also another mouth to feed. My mom had delivered a baby girl in December of 1946.

It's amazing to me how fast a woman's body can recuperate and permit her to get pregnant again after having been starved for such a long time. My sister, Marijke, was born sixteen months, almost to the day, after we were liberated from the Japanese. So, it took my mother only about seven months to recuperate from being severely undernourished to the point where she could conceive again. There were now five of us to feed, clothe, and take care of.

In the spring of 1947, we made the move to Den Haag to live with my aunt. I never really found out how this affected my grandma and grandpa who had, not too long ago, been reunited with their daughter and her family and now had to say goodbye to them again. They didn't know when they would see each other again, even though the distance wasn't that far by American standards. I don't think my grandpa had a car and going by train took about three hours one-way, was very expensive and tiring as one had to first get to the train station, either by bus or on foot, and then change trains at least once each way, take a bus or streetcar to get closer to the address they wanted to go to, and then finally walk to the house. One didn't make a trip like that too often. You might as well have moved to another country. There were not too many people who had a telephone so calling each other regularly was not an option either. Besides, calling long-distance would have been very expensive. I think it must have been a very sad day for both of my grandparents as well as for my mom.

Moving to another city may sound like a simple task, especially since there wasn't much to move. My parents hadn't bought much furniture or other belongings. After all, they had lived with my grand-parents who had all the furniture they needed. Nevertheless, moving was a big ordeal. In the Netherlands one doesn't just pick up and move whenever and wherever one wants. You first must ask and receive per-mission of the town you would like to move into before you can make the move. You must show that you have a job and/or can support your-self and your family, if you have one. The reason for this is because each city has to take care of its residents if they can't take care of themselves.

It is like Welfare in America. If you can't take care of yourself, then you go through a process by which they look at what your possibilities are and if there is enough money in their budget to take care of you. You can actually be denied the move. You also must notify the town you are moving away from that you are no longer living there. As with any bureaucratic procedure this requires a lot of paperwork and official documents and of course time and patience. However, things were a little easier in their situation since my aunt had promised to take the whole family into her apartment and promised to take care of them, if needed.

A year-and-a-half later my brother, Wouter, was born in a hospital in Scheveningen, a suburb of Den Haag. In the meantime, my father had finally found work and had obtained a position with the "Marine," where he was a secretary to one of the company leaders and arranged meetings and performed other duties. The "Marine" was a civil service job with the marines and it offered good benefits. My dad was lucky that they couldn't check out his records, as he lied about his qualifica-tions. He told them that he had graduated from high school, and that he had additional training to qualify for the job. Since a lot of records were lost with all the bombings during the war nobody could verify his qualifications. He was good when it came to selling himself though and was hired for the position. He did a great job and stayed there until he retired.

During the relatively short time we lived with my aunt I managed to twist my ankle very badly. I loved to play outside every opportunity

I had, and since we didn't have many toys my favorite thing to play with was my tennis ball. I did all kinds of stunts with it. When all you have to entertain yourself with is one ball, you get very creative. My precious ball had rolled into the street, and I ran after it. There were hardly any cars on the road yet, and no buses drove in that street. I didn't pay attention while running into the street and got run over, of all things, by a bicycle. The pain was excruciating, and the doctor was summoned to our apartment. He checked things over and decided that nothing was broken but that I had "only" twisted my ankle really bad.

Nothing was given for the pain or the swelling, not even ice packs as we didn't have a refrigerator. I had to be brave and was expected to try to walk on it as soon as possible. It hurt so terribly much that I wouldn't even try to stand on it. In desperation my parents promised me a scooter if I would walk on it while it was still hurting. I tried extremely hard to please them and walk or stand on my foot, but the pain was simply unbearable. Even thinking about the nice scooter and how much fun I would have with it, couldn't make me walk or stand. Needless to say, I didn't get a scooter. I didn't think that was fair since I didn't get anything for the pain but that's how it was. I was taught to be tough. I was extremely sad not to get the scooter since I was the only child in the neighborhood who didn't have one. How much I longed to have one of my own so I wouldn't have to beg other kids to let me use theirs.

The living arrangements with my aunt didn't work out and or last very long. I don't think she realized what she was getting into. With two families sharing one kitchen and my mother having a new baby, a sickly child, and two other children to take care of, things got quite hectic, and patience ran thin. Living like that wasn't easy under the best of circumstances but a family with four children under those conditions made it very hard indeed. Everyone really needed much more room than what my aunt was able to provide. It didn't take very long before my parents started looking for another apartment. Even though they were looking for an apartment in the same town, they had to go through the same bureaucratic red tape again.

This time though, my dad had a job, and the officials could understand why the move was needed. They found an apartment reasonably fast and not too far from my aunt's place and offered that to my parents. My mom later told me that she hadn't wanted to take that one because it was old and drafty, required a lot of work to take care of, and a lot of initial expense. Renting an apartment in the Netherlands is much like owning a house in the U.S., as one has to do all the upkeep such as painting or wall papering, putting in the floors, as well as carpeting and tiling. The only things that the landlord must maintain are the plumbing, the wiring, the roof, and the exterior painting. Even the heaters and the toilets had to be put in by the renters. My dad, however, was worried that another apartment would not be available soon and wanted to move while the opportunity was there. They lived there until the spring of 1964.

All I remember about that apartment is that it was very cold, very damp and extremely drafty, just like my mom said it would be, and it was on the third floor. It was quite roomy with a living room, dining room, three bedrooms, a kitchen and a very small room with a toilet and a little tiny sink. There was no shower or bathtub in the apartment, which wasn't unusual at all in those days. These apartments were built in the late 1920s or very early 1930s and were built very economically so more people could have a place to live. Having three bedrooms was not too nice, as we always had to share our room with another sibling. How I longed for a room of my own and not always have my sister bug me or getting into the few things I could call my own. How I enjoyed having a room of my own once I moved out!

Initially we "bathed" once a week by filling up the sink in my parent's bedroom with warm water and washed our bodies. This was alright in the summertime, but not pleasant at all in the winter as there was no heat in that room. Hair washing was done only once a month or once every six weeks, as that wasn't seen as a necessity. Your hair supposedly got cleaned when you brushed or combed it.

When we had a little more money, we could go to one of the bathhouses once a week to take a shower. One walked over there with a towel, a bar of soap, and clean underclothing. You paid the entrance fee and then you had to stand in line until it was your turn to take a shower. Everybody was told to go to the shower area and was assigned a little cubicle where you could put your clothes in. You then wrapped yourself in your towel and walked over to the shower clutching your bar of soap in your hand. You were only allowed to shower for a limited time, and then told you had to get back to your cubicle to dry off and get dressed. The next group of people was waiting their turn. In the winter we didn't wash our hair there because walking home with wet hair, even though one could cover one's head with a cap, would most certainly make one become very ill. Or so they thought and still think. I know better as I have tried out their theory in the coldest time in the winter in Alaska and didn't get a sniffle let alone become very ill.

We didn't have a water heater or central heating in our apartment, this was considered a luxury, and only enjoyed by the rich. We did have two freestanding stoves that were only used whenever we could afford to buy the coal to burn in them. One stove was in the living room and the other one in the back bedroom. That one was hardly ever used.

If my memory serves me right, we had to climb 36 steps to get upstairs to get into our apartment. Fortunately, these stairs were inside and private. Being on the third floor and having those stairs inside sometimes posed a problem, though. When someone rang the doorbell and we wanted to know who was calling on us before opening the door, we had to hang out the dining room window (which faced the street) and try to see if we recognized the visitor. If we saw who it was and wanted that person to enter, we would then run to the top of the staircase and pull on a cord which would open the door downstairs. If we didn't know the person and couldn't communicate by yelling, we had to go all the way downstairs to meet them at the door. It was a real nuisance, but it made us get lots of exercise!

Sometimes a clever salesman would do one of three things: he would pretend not to hear us yell, he would just refuse to respond to our yelling, or he wouldn't come far enough away from the door for us to see him. We diligently tried to find a way to determine who was at the door without having to run up and down the stairs, and decided to just refuse to open the door until the person would step away from the door so we could see them. It was necessary because we didn't want unpleasant situations.

Occasionally there was a spokesperson from a religious group who wouldn't leave after being told politely that we weren't interested in what he had to say. They were very persistent nevertheless in trying to save our souls. Sometimes they would go as far as not allowing us to close the door, even after we told them again and again that we weren't interested. They would put a foot in the door and keep it there until we listened to their whole pitch or until we threatened to call the police. That last option always worked even though they didn't know that we didn't even own a telephone; however, they certainly weren't going to take any chances.

The one thing I did like about the staircase was that the first ten or eleven steps from the bottom could be raised by releasing two pins. The area underneath the steps was used to store coal in the fall and winter used for heating the living room, the one and only room in the house that was heated. In the spring and summer this storage area was empty. As we got older and had bicycles, they were stored under the steps when they were not in use. They stood in the little entry way when they couldn't be stored under the steps or were parked on the boulevard against a tree. No need to worry about them getting stolen in those days!

Another problem with an upstairs apartment was that we had to be very quiet while playing inside when it was too cold or too wet to play outside. The flooring between us and the apartment below was very thin and not very soundproof. We were not allowed to run in the halls, jump around, scream or laugh loudly. The lady downstairs, who was also our landlord, became very ill and we were asked to keep as quiet as possible. We tried very hard, but she remained ill for several months until she finally died.

During the fall and winter there were many days when it was too cold to play outside. Sometimes it was just too hard to stay quiet all the time and we would make too much noise. After all, keeping four children cooped up in an upstairs apartment with hardly any toys was not an easy task. The person below would tap on the ceiling below us and make us aware that we should quiet down. It was not too bad to stay quiet when we were playing with our marbles or coloring books, but occasionally we got a severe case of cabin fever and were literally climbing the walls in the long hall that went way to the back of the house.

I climbed the walls by putting my left hand and left foot against the left wall and then the right hand and right foot against the right side of the wall. My ankles were so flexible that my feet easily bent far enough to be able to do so. The hallways weren't very wide, not as wide as the ones here in America. My ankles had to bend quite a bit, but after some practice I became very good at it and enjoyed going from one end of the hallway to the other whenever I felt like it. Even though the ceilings were higher than most houses here in America, I soon was able to climb so high that I could touch the ceiling. What fun that was!

When a severe frost was predicted we had to go downstairs and open a little trap door on the floor in the entry way and turn off the main water faucet to try to prevent the pipes from freezing. This was done late at night right before my parents went to bed. If the bicycles were in the entryway, the trap door was hard to get to. If we couldn't squeeze ourselves in such a way to reach the knob under the little trap door, we then had to move the bicycles. With so little space this was not easy. Because of that, we were sometimes asked to carry the bikes up the two flights of stairs to our room. We were also asked to store our bikes in our rooms when the weather was such that we couldn't use them for several days anyway. I would have preferred to reserve the space under the stairs for the exclusive purpose of storing the bicycles but that was not possible.

When we first moved into the apartment, my parents were still trying to catch up financially and could only afford to heat the living room. It had a freestanding stove that was fueled with coal briquettes. We children had the duty of keeping the coal bin filled up, especially at night, so it would be ready for my mom the next day. She was the one who would get up early in the morning and start the fire and would keep it going all day until she and my father went to bed. Everything was then shut off so the few embers that were still in there would soon be burned out. They seemed to know how much coal to put on, so that most of it was all burned up by the time they went to bed. They would then shake all the ashes down in the bottom to make the remaining pieces burn up faster. It also made it easier in the morning to start the fire again.

I remember that I burned a couple of small holes in the carpet one evening. My parents were away playing bridge or visiting their friends, and my older brother must have been gone too. This left me in charge of the apartment and my younger brother and sister. We kept the fire going like we were supposed to. When it came time to go to bed, I wanted to do an extra good job shaking the ashes out so my mom would be proud of me. I shook a little too hard and some of the burning coals fell on the floor in front of the stove and burned the carpet.

I was so worried about how my parents would react and wanted to hide the evidence, so I put an area rug over the spot and hoped that they wouldn't notice the burns. We then went to bed quickly, sooner than any other time when I had taken care of my brother and sister. They didn't seem to mind going to bed early as they didn't want to face our parents when they got home. Soon enough my parents came home and of course noticed the change immediately. They may not have noticed it quite as fast if we hadn't put the rug in front of the stove.

My mom came to our room ready to question us, but both my sister and I pretended to be asleep. My younger brother in the next room pretended to be asleep as well. The next morning came soon enough and to our surprise my parents were not too upset. They said they had insurance, and that the problem would be taken care of. I think they collected the money for the damaged part but never fixed it and kept the little area rug on the spot where I had put it.

Later, when finances became a little better, we were allowed to leave the door open between the living room and the dining room for half an hour or so before we ate our evening meal, which made the mealtime a much more pleasurable experience. All winter, we shivered during our meals and ate as fast as possible to be able to leave the table, wash up the dishes in the ice-cold kitchen and go back into the living room where it was warm.

The rest of the house was always cold, damp and very drafty. I always looked forward to summertime when things weren't quite so cold. It was no wonder that I had colds and sinus infections almost the entire winter, each and every year. To make things worse, we were given only one handkerchief a day, and when I had a cold, it would already be sopping wet by the time I left for school. The rest of the day I would have to blow my nose in a wet, cold handkerchief. To this day I hate the thought of blowing my nose in anything other than a Kleenex; the thought of blowing my nose in a handkerchief makes me sick. Fortunately, I don't have to use a Kleenex very often.

Because of my recurring colds and sinus infections, my tonsils were taken out when I was about 13 years old. My parents were told that that would improve my health. I have horrible memories of the supposedly minor surgery. I was operated on December 27th. The reason I remember the date is that December 25 and 26 are holidays in the Netherlands and are called First Christmas Day and Second Christmas Day. On December 27th I was taken to the hospital downtown, which was an entirely new experience for me, as I didn't remember having been in a hospital before. I had blocked out the time in the hospital while in the camp, or the time I was in the hospital right after the war. I was soon truly sorry that I submitted to this operation as I never felt so much pain in my life. But I doubt that I would have been able to talk my parents out of letting me have the surgery.

My parents figured that I was mentally too young to be in the adult ward and that I would be better off if I weren't put with people older than I was. They were able to talk the doctor into admitting me to the children's ward. Looking back, I believe I would have been much better off on the adult ward, because the staff would have been much more sympathetic.

I was all alone in my little room with glass walls which was actually a cubicle with no privacy. Nobody came in to check on me other than the nurse who had many other children to care for, and the doctor when he made his rounds. It was customary for only the immediate family to visit during specific hours and nobody under eighteen was permitted to come and see their family. This precluded any visits from my brothers and sister or from my friends from school or the neighborhood. I remember feeling very lonely, scared, and in a lot of pain.

To this day I can remember most of the operation. I was put in a big chair, and someone placed what seemed to be a giant black mask on my face. It felt horrible and made me feel like I was going to suffocate. I tried to push it away, but it was pressed harder and harder over my nose and mouth. The next thing I know is that I saw a big circle spinning, faster and faster, and getting smaller and smaller. I became very dizzy, and I must have fallen asleep soon after that. The next thing I remember is that I woke up, but the operation wasn't finished. I had woken up too early. When I opened my eyes, I saw a bowl half full with blood right under my face. The sight was terrifying. The doctor said something like, "We are almost done. We just have to cut off the uneven parts and make everything smooth." I really didn't care as I had not yet started to hurt, and I just wanted to go back to sleep. I must have done so because the next time I woke up I was more coherent and felt the most horrible pain in my throat. I couldn't speak and didn't want to, as my throat was too sore. I wanted something for the pain and gestured to the nurses to give me something when they came in or when they checked on me. I was told that I wasn't allowed to have any pain medication as I was on the children's floor of the hospital and children didn't get anything for the pain when they had their tonsils taken out. I was told I could have ice cream and cold drinks, but I refused those because I thought that swallowing anything, even something cold was going to be too painful. They told me that it would diminish the pain, but I didn't want to believe them. How could that be? I went home a day or so later and within 48 hours had a severe earache. I had gotten an ear infection on New Year's Eve just a few days after my operation. The doctor was called and came to the house even though it was a holiday. I must have gotten some kind of medication because I got better fast after that.

My younger brother didn't fare much better in the cold, drafty apartment either. Every winter he looked pale and sickly and stayed that way until spring when the sun came out to dry out the dampness and warm up everything. My older brother and my younger sister seemed to always be more plump and healthier than my younger brother and I. We were the "kasplantjes" or hothouse plants needing extra care and concern.

My mom would try so hard to find anything to help us grow better and be sick less often. When we were a little older, she was told that cod liver oil would help us do better during the winter. Every day of every month that had the letter "r" in it we were given a spoonful of cod liver oil. The only one who liked it was my sister and she got a big kick out of reminding my mom that the month of August was almost over and that she should buy the bottle of cod liver oil and have it ready. Oh, how we hated that.

Later, my mom was told that eating live yeast every day is good for a person. So, she walked over to the bakery every morning and bought a clump of fresh yeast. When we came home for lunch there would be an open-faced sandwich waiting for us with a thick layer of yeast on it covered with a thin layer of jam. If we arrived home a little later than we should have, the jam and the yeast would have started to work, and the sandwich would be all bubbly. It not only looked horrible, but it smelled and tasted horrible as well. But we had to get it down so we would grow big and strong.

We were probably much better off taking the cod liver oil. At least we could swallow it down in one gulp and eat a cracker or a slice of bread after it to get rid of the taste. When I got tested for allergies in the 1980s, guess what I was allergic to? Yeast!

As I mentioned earlier, we had no hot running water, no shower or bathtub, and none of the other conveniences like a washing machine, a refrigerator, or a telephone that make life easier today. Dishwashers were unheard of in households unless the people were very, very wealthy.

My mom had to do all the laundry herself without a washing machine. Mondays were washday, not an easy day for her. She would start by heating big kettles of water on the kitchen stove and boiling some of the wash such as sheets and other cottons. If she wanted to rinse the wash with warm water, she would have to boil more water to mix with the ice-cold water out of the tap. After the wash was clean and rinsed, she would hang it up outside on the balcony off the back bedroom until it was dry. Sometimes it would hang there for days because the cold would freeze the doors to the balcony shut and we couldn't bring in the wash.

Other times, we would help bring in the wash, which was as stiff as a board, and we had to drape it over the furniture to thaw it out or hang it on drying racks in front of the stove in the living room until my dad got home. He didn't want to see anything like that in the living room, so we had to move all the wash to different bedrooms to continue drying. In the wintertime my mom's hands were always cracked and dry, and sometimes the cracks were so deep that they would bleed at the slightest touch. No matter how much cream she put on her hands, they stayed that way until summertime. When the wash was finally dry, everything was ironed and neatly put away. We didn't change sheets very often. Our clothes, socks and underwear were all worn several times before being washed. In fact, I remember that we only got clean underwear and clean socks once a week unless they got dirty somehow and our sheets were changed only once a month.

My mom had to go on foot to purchase all the groceries. There were no supermarkets where she could select all she needed in one trip. Even if such a market had existed, she couldn't have possibly carried everything for a family of six.

Every day, she walked to the milk store for her milk, cheese and eggs, and brought those groceries home. Then she went to the bakery for her bread and took that home, and finally she went to the vegetable store. The first few years we couldn't afford to eat any meat or fish so that saved a trip to the butcher or the fish store.

I remember her buying raw milk at first and later milk in bottles. Raw milk was cheaper, and with all the milk drinkers in the house it made enough difference to buy it that way. The milk had to be boiled before we drank it, which was no problem for my mom as she believed that drinking warm milk was better anyway, especially in the winter. I didn't particularly care for warm milk, but I had to drink it that way. Cold milk on a cold day, is not good for you, I was told.

The milk that came in bottles was not homogenized and had an aluminum cap on the top of the bottle. You could peel back the top ever so carefully and take little sips out of it. Since the milk wasn't homogenized, the cream floated on the top. To me that was the best part of the milk, and I always took a little sip out of the bottle on the way back from the store. What a treat it was and how much I enjoyed the taste of the creamier milk. Occasionally, I accidentally drank too much and got caught. That would mean a beating with the rug beater or my mom's hands, which was not a pleasant experience, but it didn't seem to stop me from doing it again the next day. Pretty soon I learned how much I could drink and get away with.

For breakfast we would get "havermoutpap" (oatmeal cooked in milk and sugar and the consistency of pudding). Boy did I like that! My mother made it nice and sweet. I still like it cooked that way and will eat that whenever I'm visiting my family abroad. I sometimes still cook it like that for myself. It tastes so much better than the way Americans cook their oatmeal. I can't understand why one would cook oatmeal in water and make it so thick that you can cut it with a knife, and then you put cold milk on it and somehow get some of the warm oatmeal and some of the cold milk on your spoon. What a mess!! Today "havermoutpap" comes ready to eat in bottles. You don't even have to cook it anymore and you can eat it cold or warmed up in the microwave.

Other days we would get bread with peanut butter or jam. We were allowed to have two slices of bread with some sort of spread on it. If we wanted more bread, which we always did, we could have salt or sugar on it. Or, when it was available, we put solidified bacon drippings on the bread. We put salt on that as well as the bacon hadn't been salted. For lunch we ate the same thing during the winter.

I was always happy to see spring and summer approaching. Not only did we get some fresh produce which I looked forward to, but we could also sit on the balcony and look down into other people's little backyards. How I longed to have a yard, and how I envied those people. I wished that we had a little yard where I could sit while reading my books, and we would also have a little garden and grow things like produce and flowers. And there would also be many birds that would sit in the trees and bushes and sing their beautiful songs.

When the fresh produce became available in the stores, we would get a few slices of tomato or cucumber on our bread. We usually put some salt on the tomato but sometimes we put sugar on it, depending what kind of mood we were in. On the cucumber we would always sprinkle some salt. In the summer we would often get buttermilk. When there was some extra money, my mother would add crushed strawberries, fresh currants or raspberries, and some sugar. We didn't have a blender or juicer, so she just stirred it all together. We always looked forward to that a lot as we remembered from year to year how good it tasted and how much we wished we could have it in the other seasons as well. I also liked the different color after berries were in there. It seemed to brighten up the whole meal.

One thing never failed though. As soon as I had a few strawberries in my system I would break out in huge hives that itched something fierce. The only thing I ever remember getting for the itch was cold buttermilk packs, but I don't think they helped a whole lot as I remember being in agony very often. There were no available at that time. I could never understand how something that tasted so good, like berries, could have such a negative effect on me. Every year I hoped that it would be different, that this year I wouldn't have any bad reaction. I was the only one in my family who had allergies and I didn't understand that either. Why me?

We didn't know much about allergies in those days and were told that one outgrows them, so every year I was instructed to eat the berries, or whatever had given me the reaction before, to see what happened. I finally stopped getting such big hives, but later in life my allergies would cause me to have serious breathing problems.

For supper we would have potatoes, vegetables, and pudding for dessert. We didn't have money for meat, fish or any other type of protein with our evening meal. We would have plates full of potatoes, either mashed or just cooked with meat broth over it. We didn't have thick gravy like you could get in the USA; broth with the fat floating on top and all the drippings from the bottom of the gravy boat. In the winter we would get "stamppot" which consisted of mashed potatoes mixed with sauerkraut, kale or mashed carrots in it.

Sometimes I just scooped the fat from the top and poured it all over my potatoes. At other times I tried hard to get more drippings than anything else. If no broth was available, my mother would melt margarine and add a cube of concentrated meat broth (thicker than bouillon and darker in color) and we would use that to pour over our potatoes.

In the wintertime we each got one apple a day. They had wonderful very tart and very firm apples called "goudreinetten," which I always looked forward to having. A lot of people cooked them and made applesauce from them. I preferred them whole and raw and green. I couldn't understand why anybody would want to spoil something that is so perfect by cooking it and making it soft and mushy. Sadly, they were only available in the winter.

As time went by and things slowly became a little better for our family, we would get a small serving of meat once a week on Sundays and later some fish on Fridays as well. Eventually we got one fried egg for breakfast on Sunday morning with a little bit of bacon. I think that I must have eaten mostly vegetarian the first ten years of my life. Generally, I thought this way of eating was all right, except that we had way too much sugar and salt in our diet and maybe too much fat.

At one point, my younger brother had to cut back on salt as he already showed signs of high blood pressure and my sister had so many cavities that she had to have fillings put in all her teeth, not very long after she got her permanent teeth. She even had fillings in her baby teeth. However, my teeth were very strong, much to the surprise of all the dentists I have seen over the years. To this day, I still don't have any false teeth.

Getting groceries for such a large family was hard enough during the week but getting them on Saturdays or days that fell before holidays was even more difficult. All the grocery stores were closed on Sunday and holidays, and most of them also closed on Saturday afternoon. My mother had to carry groceries for six people for a minimum of two days and sometimes three or four days. All of us were big eaters, and when you eat very little or no meat or protein, you have to fill up on staples such as potatoes or noodles. Potatoes must have been cheap because we ate those a lot, but they were very heavy to carry.

We didn't have a refrigerator or icebox and all the food, including the milk, had to be reheated daily to prevent spoiling. After several days of being boiled, the milk would turn yellow and had a thick tough peel on it. Nobody wanted to have that part, nor did we enjoy drinking the milk once it got so yellowed. Sometimes we would get hot chocolate made from cocoa powder, sugar, and milk. I soon figured out just how little was needed to make a good cup of hot chocolate and ate some of the chocolate mixture before the hot milk was added to it. I was already in love with chocolate any way I could get it.

Since we were in school on Saturday morning and my father worked until noon, my mother had to carry all the groceries back home by herself. Later, when the work week shortened and we were home on Saturday mornings as well, we would all help carry the groceries for her. We didn't mind going to the stores with her, but when the weather was nice, we would rather have played outside. Also, standing in line in the stores and making sure that other people wouldn't cut in line was not much fun. Sometime big arguments started, and women yelled that they were there first, and then others would say that "they were there first." You were usually taken advantage of if you were a child and were buying something without an adult with you. The women would say that they had come into the store before you were there, and since children didn't or couldn't argue with adults then, there wasn't much that could be done. Sometimes the storeowner would know when I had come in, with or without my sister or brother, and would keep track of who came after me. If an argument arose, he would take our side. We didn't need to worry about our turn if my mother was with us as she kept track and wouldn't allow anyone to go ahead of her. Much later that problem was solved as you had to pull a number when you entered the store and that way there was no arguing about who got there first.

When we came home from school, my mother was always there waiting for us with a cup of tea and a "bescuitje," a very cheap cookie that didn't taste too bad. Even young children got a cup of tea although their tea was weaker and had more sugar in it. In the wintertime she would sometimes make fresh homemade soup on the stove in the living room. Her tomato soup was out of this world! We could smell it as soon as we opened the door at the bottom of the steps. We would run upstairs to be even closer to the smell and to have the warm, tasty soup. I could have eaten that every day. When my mom had free time (I am amazed that she ever had any), she would make homemade cookies or a pie from scratch. These were special treats, and we certainly looked forward to eating them.

While she asked us about our day in school, she would continue her mending or sewing projects. With so many people in the house and no money to buy anything new unless absolutely necessary, there was a lot of mending to do. She even mended the holes in the toes and heels of our socks. The toes weren't so bad when they were mended as there was usually enough room in the shoe to make up the difference in thickness. The heel, however, was another matter. If my mother had to use thicker yarn than the original, which often was the case, we would end up with blisters on our heels because of the rubbing. However, she did a beautiful job, and although it always looked very nice, it just wasn't very comfortable. And, of course, I got teased in school when the kids found out that I had socks on that had been repaired by my mother. They never had to endure that. When their socks got a hole in it, they got new ones.

Even nylon stockings got repaired when they had a run in them. The lady who fixed the stockings charged according to the width of the run and the size of the holes. If the stockings weren't too badly damaged, it was cheaper to have her repair them than to buy new ones. I still remember the machine she used to repair the nylon stockings. I was fascinated by the way the stockings looked after the repair and had great admiration for the tedious job she did. There was absolutely no evidence that there ever had been a run or a hole in the stockings because she matched the thread color with the color of the stockings perfectly.

As we got bigger, we had to help around the house more and more. My mom didn't have any help, and the apartment was large and required a lot of work to keep clean. It seemed that we needed to spend so much time cleaning the house. I definitely didn't enjoy it or wanted to do it so often. I knew it was a useless task because everything became dirty again so quickly.

I especially hated cleaning the stairs. That was a big job, and we didn't have a radio or anything else to listen to while we worked. I do think it was fair for my mom to ask us to help, as she never had any time for herself otherwise, but that didn't make us like the chores any better. However, when the weather was nice enough to be outside, she would reward us with trips to the dunes or the beach in the summer so we could play in the sand and have a change of scenery. I'm sure she didn't care about going there herself since she always had to worry about getting sunburned. She had a very fair complexion and burned easily. We always made sure that she could sit in a shady place. Later in life she developed skin cancer on her nose as did many women who had been in the camps. We did enjoy those outings, simple as they were. I often brought a book to read, and we brought glass bottles filled with tap water along as there were not too many places where you could get a drink of water for free and plastic bottles were not available at that time. We had to be very careful not to drop the bottles in the street. When we got to the dunes or to the beach, we would dig a hole big enough to put the bottle in to keep it cool. We had no ice cubes or ice-cold water to begin with.

In the winter my mom took us to a little pond nearby to attempt to ice skate. We didn't have fancy skates with shoes on them. Ours tied to our boots or shoes and always came untied the minute you twisted your ankle. Since I had very weak ankles, I would spend most of the time sitting at the side retying my skates. But no matter how cold it was or how much time I spent sitting on the sidelines tying my skates, it was much better than staying inside. However, I never did learn to ice skate, nor did I ever feel I wanted to.

Eventually things became a little easier for my mom. We had our milk, eggs and cheese delivered to our house, so she didn't have to carry them back from the store. For a while we continued to buy raw milk. We put an empty pan on the bottom step as well as a note listing other items we needed that day. Raw milk was much cheaper and all of us liked milk and had to drink three or four glasses a day. As the milkman filled the order, one of us would run down with the money to pay. If my mother didn't have the money to pay that day, he would run a tab. We would then bring back up as much as we could carry. Sometimes it took more than one trip.

Later, we were able to afford milk in bottles delivered to our house. We had to put the old bottles down on the steps, so we didn't get charged for them again. There was enough deposit on all glass bottles to make sure we gave back the old ones. I always liked to drink some when it came fresh out of the bottle, as it was so nice and white. Since we never had a means of keeping our milk cold, we always ended up with boiled milk that just didn't taste as good.

Because of our financial state, we were always much worse off than most of the other kids in my school, so we never had any new clothes or shoes. Initially, we received most of our clothing from the Salvation Army. I remember my mother telling me one time that the next day I was going to get some new shoes. How happy and excited I was thinking that I would get "new" shoes. I had never had new shoes; I just imagined how it would feel to have shoes on that nobody else had worn yet and were all mine. I told all the other kids in school about it, but they somehow knew better and told me they didn't believe it. The next day came and off I went with my mother to pick up my new shoes. I was so excited and skipped instead of walking, and hardly touched the ground with each step I took. All I could think of was the pretty new shoes I would soon have.

I soon found out though that we didn't go to the shoe store but to the Salvation Army where we picked out the best-fitting used shoes they could find for me. They didn't even look new at all and I'm sure they weren't the best-fitting shoes for my feet. My heart sank: I can still feel the disappointment and hurt. I wondered how I could have been so stupid to think that we would have money for new shoes for me. Why would I get new shoes? My brothers and sister hadn't had new shoes yet so why should I? Somehow, I thought that this time it would be different. Why hadn't I believed the other kids? I worried about how were they going to react?

When I got up the next day I really didn't want to go to school. How could I avoid my schoolmates? How could I avoid their teasing? But I had to go to school; there was just no way of escaping it. Besides, I would have to face them eventually. They all wanted to see my brand-new shoes. Oh, how I got teased when they saw the "new" shoes on my feet. What could I say other than to admit that they were right?

When I was a little older, we got a few more new clothes, and more often. My mother knew how to knit, and she would knit up a storm every fall and winter. She did a great job! She even knitted us special hats through which we girls could pull our ponytails. They were cute, and I don't think anyone else had hats like that. Also, she was able to take some sewing courses, and not only learned how to sew clothes from a pattern, but how to draw the patterns as well. This saved the cost of buying patterns, plus the clothes would fit much better than they would have otherwise.

She made some beautiful clothes for us, and we liked them even better if we were allowed to pick out the material and the colors. However, what we got to pick out had to be what my mother liked too and unfortunately her taste was not at all like ours. We liked more bright colors with stripes or plaids or figures on it but she liked the more subdued and darker color prints. We almost never got any store-bought clothes like the other kids in school had, but at least they weren't used, and they were more in fashion than the ones we had worn so far.

CHAPTER 5

My brothers, sister, and I went to a Catholic school because of an agreement my parents had made with my aunt with whom we lived initially in Den Haag. She was a devout Catholic and had told my parents that we could all live with her until they were able to get back on their feet, but only if their children were baptized and raised Catholic. Only out of necessity did my parents agree to my aunt's conditions.

My mother had been raised a Lutheran and my father a Catholic. Neither was attending church any longer. My father had been excommunicated because of his divorce from his first wife. In the 1930s divorce wasn't accepted in the Catholic Church and therefore a second marriage was not acceptable. So, my mother wasn't really acknowledged by his family as his wife, but only as a girlfriend, especially by one of my aunts who had been raised in the convent and later took her vows as a nun. This meant that, according to the Catholic Church, we were born out of wedlock. Fortunately, my parents had been married in the court house so in that respect we were legally their children. It wasn't a good situation, though as we had to master all the things you learn growing up Catholic without the support or examples to follow at home. I don't even remember our aunt being a role model or helping us with questions we might have had.

Initially, we (the children) studied the Bible and went to church because we wanted to and felt some kind of need. We liked the stories in the Bible and believed, as gullible as we were, everything that was told us. As we got older and saw things from different angles, things didn't look the same and we stopped going to church.

First, it was very hard to attend church and know what was going on. The entire Mass, except for the sermon, was spoken in Latin. Granted we had our missal, a book where all the spoken text was printed in Latin and Dutch, that we could follow once we could read fast enough to keep up, but only if we could hear what was being said. We sometimes came early enough to find a seat near the front of the church so we could hear but we were soon told to leave those seats by church members who claimed that we were sitting in their seat. I don't know if there was any truth to it as in those days children were always told things like that just so adults could sit where they wanted or get their way. Since my parents didn't go to church and we didn't have any other role models we didn't know if they were telling the truth. So, we just obeyed them and vacated the seat. We often ended up standing in the back of the church and had a hard time hearing the sermon.

At other times we arrived at church just after the church bell rang the last time and the services had already started. Later, we told our parents that we were going to church, but we just played outside. It was a great excuse for us to get out of the house for a couple of hours and do what we wanted to do without any adults looking over our shoulders. We always got some money to put in the bucket when they came by for contributions. Initially we were good children and put our money in the bucket. After a while we decided that the church didn't do anything for us so why give them the money. There was a store nearby that sold French fries and that was open on Sundays. This was very unusual as most businesses were closed on Sunday. How we looked forward to our treat. When the weather was nice, we would go to a park and play or find an empty field and pick flowers for my mother. We always seemed to come up with a nice bouquet of wild-flowers from some field that was nearby. When we got home my father often asked what the sermon was about and since we didn't know we would make up something. I'm sure he had his suspicions about where we were especially when we came home with a bouquet of flowers, but he asked anyway and never really questioned us very long. He probably didn't care one way or another but wanted to pretend he was doing his job and raising his children the right way.

When the weather was not very nice, we would go to church but leave after the sermon, so we had some idea what the priest had talked about. When the weather was cold, we would go and stand in the back of the church on the heat registers. We wouldn't even try to find a place to sit because standing over or near the registers was warmer than sitting in the front of the church. If the sermon was interesting, we would try harder to listen, but usually we found other ways to entertain ourselves. One diversion was to take a big sheet of paper, tear it up in little pieces, and release them in the air right above the register to see how high the blower sent them into the church. Finally, we quit going altogether.

My father wasn't too thrilled about us going to Catholic school anyway. Unlike in America going to a parochial school in the Netherlands didn't necessarily mean that you would get a better education. But unlike here it was free and therefore affordable to all. Our attending that school meant constant reminders to us of something that he didn't really care about.

The Catholics didn't help us at all, especially financially. My father often wondered whatever happened to sharing one's resources with people who are worse off than you are. The priest made several visits a year to the house and tried to persuade my parents to have more children, (i.e., more souls to be raised Catholic). When my father asked the priest if the church would help finance more children, he was turned down. In fact, the priest was rather surprised that he would even think of asking such a thing. Never mind that he lived in a warm house and was living much more comfortably than we were.

My father also hadn't forgotten the incident in the camp when my mother smuggled bacon into the camp at the request of the nuns in the hospital and was turned down when she asked for a few pieces for us.

However, he kept his word, and we stayed in Catholic school through my sixth grade.

There were several things that bothered my parents about the Catholic school system. The schools were segregated, which meant that the boys and the girls couldn't be in the same school. My parents found this principle to be absolutely uncalled for. In Indonesia both sexes played and learned together. My parents didn't see the value of keeping boys and girls separated while in school. Also, the girls' school had a dress code while the boys' school didn't seem to have one. We didn't have to wear uniforms, as nobody had money for that. Most people were still trying to catch up with what they had lost in the war. The dress code for the girls meant that they weren't allowed to wear slacks in the winter unless they wore a skirt or a dress over them. First, we didn't know that and second, we didn't have the luxury of wearing that many clothes in one day. So, the first cold day I went to school in slacks with some kind of sweater over it, but I was sent home during morning recess to change into proper attire. My father was furious, to say the least. I guess he wasn't only upset over such a stupid rule, but about the fact that his little girl was sent home in the middle of the morning. What if my mother hadn't been home because of all the grocery shopping she had to do daily? He was ready to take us out of that school but still didn't have much choice at that time. At least he didn't think so. Finally, though, something happened that made him decide that he had enough.

One day, my oldest brother, who was probably about fifteen years old, was supposed to pick up my sister and me after school. The school was built kind of like a fort with all the classrooms situated around a big square where the playground was located and used for recess before and after school. We had to go through a couple of open doorways to get onto the playground.

My brother was supposed to wait outside of the doorways, but he made the mistake of going through the doorways to wait for us in the playground. This meant that he now was able to mingle with the girls which was a big no-no. He was punished for that by the nuns and had to write 100 times, "I shall never trespass on the girls' playground again." My father was infuriated about this incident and that apparently was the straw that broke the camel's back. We all were transferred to public schools after that incident. This transfer happened at the end of my sixth grade, and since my parents still presumed that I wasn't ready to take the entrance exam to be admitted to high school, they signed me up to repeat the sixth grade — this time in a public school very close to home.

I don't have too many happy memories of the Catholic school either. One of my first significant memories was either in kindergarten or first grade. Once, during that year, the nuns took all of us to the furnace room which was the source of heat for the entire school. It was very warm in there, much warmer than I liked. We were told to stand really close to the furnace and stay close together. Then the huge door to the furnace was opened and we had to come even closer so that we could feel the intense heat and see the huge flames up close. When the nuns were satisfied that we had a good impression of the fire we were told that that's what hell was like, and that we would certainly end up there if we didn't behave in class and obey the teacher. The teachers must not have been able to keep the classroom orderly without that threat.

Memories of the heat must have triggered my memories of the concentration camps because I felt very frightened. I seemed to have been more scared by that experience than the other girls who thought it was sort of scary, but also sort of entertaining. That night, when my parents asked us about school, I was too scared to tell them what happened. I was worried that somehow, I would get punished because I must have done something wrong for them to do this to us. My father had a hard hand and a big hand, and I was very afraid of it.

Besides the episode with my clothes and the times I had to stand in front of the class for talking or whatever little mischief I had got into. I probably wasn't paying attention to what was going on as I found whatever they were talking about very boring or of no use of knowing.

Anyway, I was told by the teacher that I was a terrible child, and all the children better take a good look at this terrible child. I didn't think I was such a terrible child, and I sure didn't feel good about being told I was a terrible child. Another time I had to have some kind of paper signed by my parents. I don't know exactly what it was for, but it was about something I would have been punished for. The next day I "forgot" to bring the signed paper to school hoping the teacher would not remember about it. Of course, she remembered and told me that I had to bring it the next day or else I would be in even more trouble. I forged my mother's signature hoping that the teacher wouldn't notice. She noticed right away and now I was in even more trouble, not only with her, but with my parents as well.

All through grade school I was teased a lot because I just didn't fit in and wasn't able to defend myself. I so hated being teased, and the only way I knew how to try to stop the teasing was to bite and kick. This is the kind of behavior you see in very young children who don't know how to express their feelings any other way yet. But I was still doing this in third or fourth grade, obviously way past the normal development stage. The nuns didn't quite know what to do with me, of course, as this behavior wasn't tolerated. Their punishment consisted of making me stand in the corner of the room after I was told again in front of the rest of the class what a horrible child I had been. At the end of the day, they would send me home with a letter to my parents which resulted in punishment by them. There must have been other unpleasant memories as well because I do remember that I was very happy to leave that school.

In the Netherlands there is no separate school for junior or senior high school. When you are done with grade school, you go to one of the many different categories of high school (a school of higher learning). It takes anywhere from three to six years to obtain a diploma, depending on the program. One must pass a national test to get admitted into one of the schools that is a pre-college type.

My parents told the new sixth grade teacher that they wanted me to go to the kind of high school which would be preparation for higher education. But they were sure that I would need lots of extra help to pass the test as I wasn't all that smart. Fortunately, I had a nice teacher that year that saw much more in my abilities than anyone else ever had before and she knew how to bring out the best in me. She found out where I needed extra help and where I just needed more confidence. She tutored me after school, when necessary, and because of her I passed with flying colors. She would have had my vote for the teacher of the year award because she helped me in other ways as well.

Studying for the entrance exam to get into high school was a very trying time for me. I had to compete not only with the other kids in my class but with all the sixth graders in my country. If I didn't pass it, I would have to repeat sixth grade again or go to a lower-level high school, the kind of school my parents didn't want me to attend because most of the kids enrolled there would come from blue-collar families. We were a white-collar family my father said and "don't you ever forget it!" Never mind that we had less money or other material things than most of the blue-collar families. I didn't understand this class difference — to me people were people.

So, I had to cram and cram for my exams, and remember a great deal of what I would now call useless information. It was useless because it was all just facts rather than the how and why, which I found more meaningful. For example, in history we had to remember pages and pages of dates concerning when wars started, who was at war with whom, and when they ended. Or who and when a Prince became King of what country, whom he married, and who his kids were. There was nothing about why the wars started, what took place and why they finally ended. That information came later and even then, it was not as elaborate as I would have liked it to be.

In geography class I had to remember all the countries in the world and their colonies and all the capitals. I also had to memorize what was found in these countries like gold, spices, or other valuable resources. We even had to learn about mountain passes and "polders" which are bodies of land in the Netherlands surrounded by dikes, so they won't flood. Even though it was very hard for me to learn those, I liked that subject much better as I could dream of all those far away and romantic places. They all sounded much better than where I lived.

In math class we had to memorize the multiplication tables up to twenty. You had to know (in your head, no piece of paper was allowed) multiplications such as 18 times 19, etc., at the snap of a finger. Then there was a subject called "hoofdrekenen" which meant that I had to be able to add and subtract, again in my head, the calculations the teacher gave me. She might give ten additions and subtractions in a row and when she was finished, one had to be able to come up with the right answer. These were not just single-digit numbers; they could be, and often were, up to three digits long. I had to study, study, and study. I had a really hard time with math as it was all very abstract. In fact, when I first had to learn to add or multiply, I had to have tutoring from by a friend of my parents who would spend a couple hours each week trying to make me understand the "how and the why." She took marbles, peas or whatever she had at hand, and she showed me what happened when multiplication or addition took place by placing them on the table. Once she showed me how to think and count like that, things made much more sense to me. I also had a hard time trying to remember or understand things like dikes, dams, or mountain passes just by explanation in the books. There were very few illustrations in textbooks and to just talk about how a dam was built was mind boggling to me. The same problem arose with a simple task like setting the table. I had to go to each place setting to make sure the forks, knives and spoons were in the right place; in other words, I couldn't do it from one side and put the silverware on the other side of the table without walking around the table.

Anyway, my mother would drill me after school, after supper, and often even make me get up an hour earlier in the morning to drill me again. I usually didn't do very well so early in the morning, and that resulted in my mom yelling at me and I became more stressed. Often, we both ended up crying. She would cry because she didn't understand how hard it was for me and I cried because I didn't think I would ever be able to learn everything I was told I needed to learn to pass that exam.

I became more and more nervous as the test day approached. It was during this time that I started sleepwalking. I did not just walk around the house from room to room. I often ended up outside in the street. This was very dangerous, as I had to walk down those 36 steps in the dark. Once outside I was very confused. Why did the other people have regular clothes on while I was wearing pajamas? Lucky for me I always seemed to end up waking up shortly after I got out in the street, probably because of the colder temperature. I don't remember ever shutting the door behind me. I don't want to think about what might have happened if I had shut the door. I could have easily kept on walking on the busiest street in town and been run over. My parents never seemed to wake up until I was already outside, yet I had to walk right by their room before going down the stairs. They must have been heavy sleepers as the steps creaked when I walked on them. They finally found out somehow and put another lock on the door that was so high that I could not reach it even on my tiptoes. When I tried to open the door, while sleepwalking, I became very frustrated at not being able to open the door and that would wake me up. The sleepwalking stopped almost instantly once I had taken my exam and found out that I had passed after all. Soon summer vacation started, and I have never walked in my sleep since then.

The teacher, who helped me get ready for my test, also helped me overcome my fear of water. We had to take mandatory swimming lessons during school time. I was scared to death of water, so much so that I didn't want to go into the swimming pool and cried, in front of all the kids, when I was told I had to. All I had to do was walk into the wading pool. It was no big deal, as it wasn't very deep. But to me it was very scary, and I didn't want to go into that pool for any reason.

Finally, she talked to me and tried to reassure me that everything was going to be all right and that nothing bad was going to happen. No matter how much she tried to reassure me I still wasn't convinced that I wanted to go in. Finally, she promised me that I would get a fresh apple fritter every time I would go in and try my best. Since there was never too much food in our house, and not something special like apple fritters, I promised her that I would try it just once. It was scary because during one of the first lessons we had to dunk our heads under the water. What a terrifying idea. How could one breathe? But the teacher kept her promise each time I kept mine. She would go to the bakery while we were swimming and when I got back my fresh apple fritter would be waiting for me. I don't seem to remember how the other kids reacted to my getting this kind of treatment, but it must have been all right.

Slowly, but surely, I grew less and less afraid of the water. The time came when I had to learn to swim in the deep end. How could it be possible to not sink to the bottom of that deep pool? How long would it be before I would drown? And what happens when you drown? Do you sink to the bottom of the pool and stay there? Most of the time you couldn't even see the bottom, as the water was all cloudy. But for the kids like me, a stick was hung over the water and at the end of the stick was a big loop. We had to drape our bodies in the hoop and the teacher would hold it in such a way that we were floating in the water. Eventually I felt confident enough to try without the loop. How proud I was.

By the end of the school year, I could swim well enough to try out for my first swimming diploma — diploma A. This involved jumping in the deep end of the pool and swimming a certain number of laps doing the breaststroke immediately followed by a certain number of laps on my back making sure that my hands were on my waist. I couldn't use them to paddle with. If that part of the test was passed, one then had to jump into the deep end of the pool again and tread water for five minutes without having the head or the hands under the water. It sure was a funny sight, seeing heads bobbing and hands above the water. I passed without any problems! Today, I would feel like there was really something missing in my life if I haven't been able to swim for a while. I love it! This was my first major accomplishment to help me feel a little bit better about myself. I not only passed the national entrance exam but got over my fear of water, learned to swim, and even learned to dive.

That summer my mother could afford to let us go swimming most afternoons. We were excited as it got us out of the house. The whole outing took up most of our afternoon as we first had to walk to the pool which was at least a mile away. Then we had to stand in line and wait our turn. Every hour on the hour the next bunch of people, mostly kids, were allowed to walk to the dressing rooms. Since there were only a certain number of dressing rooms, they would only allow a limited number of people to go in the swimming area. When our turn finally came, we changed quickly into our swimming suits and got into the water. About fifteen minutes before the hour was up, the whistle blew, and we all had to leave the water and change back into our street clothes. It also gave the janitors a chance to quickly dry the floors in each dressing area as best as they could. The total time we were in the water was maybe thirty minutes or so, but we were happy as it was a different way of spending our afternoons.

This was our reward for helping our mom with the housework all morning. Sometimes we were given a nickel or dime to buy a big sour pickle or pickled onion afterwards. There were no chips or other snacks to be bought. We sure looked forward to our treat. It wasn't long after we started swimming regularly that somebody taught me how to dive. A whole new world opened and before long I enjoyed picking up objects from the bottom of the pool. I sure had come a long way from being afraid to put my head under the water to retrieving things from the bottom of the deep end of the pool. Anyway, this wasn't always as easy as one would expect as the bottom of the pool was often not visible due to the cloudy water. The water in the pool wasn't kept all that clean and I am surprised that we didn't get all kinds of diseases. One thing I did get quite often was athlete's feet. We didn't get to shower before or after getting into the pool, and I guess nobody had told me how important it is to thoroughly dry between the toes. I remember how red and sore they got especially when the skin peeled several layers deep. We didn't get anything to get rid of it. I don't know if there was even anything available for athlete's feet at that time. But all my life while growing up I had the impression that I had to be tough and bear it. Once we quit going to the swimming pool, the athlete's feet healed only to come back the next summer when we started swimming again.

My school years were stressful in many other ways as well. I was still held back a lot by my parents. They thought that anything extra would be too tiring for me and therefore didn't allow me to participate in any activities outside of the school. This meant that I could not join the Girl Scouts in grade school or go to birthday parties if they were not during the weekend. There was also another program for kids who lived upstairs or who did not have a backyard and who wanted to learn about gardening.

The city also made available little postage size plots for use by kids like us. Once a week they would all walk over to their little plots and spend a couple of hours first preparing the dirt for the planting of flowers and vegetables, and later planting a nice little garden. The next day they would talk about what they had been doing, how their garden was coming along, and how much fun they had. How I envied them, and how I wondered why that much fun would be too tiring for me. I also wondered why it was all right for me to carry groceries home for my mom and walk for many blocks with the heavy bags over my shoulder or in my arms. I knew I did other things around the house that required strength and energy. Maybe they figured that I wouldn't have any more energy left or be too worn out after doing all the chores at home.

I remember feeling very lonely because I didn't have anything in common with the other children. They seemed so different from me. They knew how to play and to have fun. Learning how to read or do anything else didn't appear that hard for them. They were talking about things I knew nothing about — relatives, going to visit grandparents, going on trips across town or even to another town, and talking on the telephone. These were all things that may have seemed normal to them but were very alien to me. We didn't have any extra money to take the streetcar or bus, let alone take a train to visit any relatives that lived out of town. All my relatives, except my one aunt, lived out of town. For the longest time I didn't even think I had any relatives since we never saw any or heard much about them. When we did hear about them, I somehow didn't make the connection that they were my family. For example, if my parents were talking about one of their relatives and they only used a first name, I wouldn't always understand that the person being discussed was related. Only much later, did I find out everybody has two sets of grandparents.

I never knew my grandparents on my father's side because he was an orphan. His parents had both died when he was a little boy due to unknown circumstances. The Catholics raised him and his sisters. The people I called "Opa" (grandpa) and "Oma" (grandma) were from my mother's side of the family. My Opa was my real grandpa but his wife, whom we called Oma, was really the sister of my real grandmother. My real grandmother had died, and my grandfather had married her sister. This was very confusing to me for the longest time as I addressed them as Oma and Opa while my mother called these same people "father" and "aunt."

To make matters even more confusing, I was supposed to call the few friends my parents visited regularly "aunt and uncle," even though they weren't really any relation to us at all. This was customary. Instead of calling somebody who was a good friend of your parents Mr. or Mrs. you would call them uncle or aunt. So, when I found out that they weren't real family I was very disappointed. These were friendly, fun people who always treated us kids nicely and tried to help us whenever they could.

While in grade school, during weekends and summer vacations, I was allowed to play outside in the neighborhood. Playing outside was lots of fun even though we didn't have many toys to play with. We played in a side street which was safe as there were hardly any cars coming through it. I usually had a tennis ball which I threw across the street trying to hit the curb so that the ball would bounce back to me. When I was lucky, I had two or three balls which I would throw against a brick wall trying to learn to juggle them. When I got better at that I would throw them up in the air and eventually I was able to juggle three balls easily. I also worked on trying to juggle with four balls, and to juggle three balls using only one hand. I hula-hooped for long periods of time, played marbles trying to get better so I wouldn't lose so many times. However, I never got good at marbles and ended up with a flat thumbnail from shooting marbles so hard.

When there were more kids, we would play hide and seek, tag, hopscotch, or jump rope. We also played with tops and played leap-frog. Sometimes we had eight or nine kids all lined up with some space in between each other and we would leap-frog over the whole row, then bend over to be the last one to be jumped over. When we first started doing it everybody would bend down as far as they could but as we got better, we all raised our bodies higher which made it more of a challenge. Playing with our tops was also fun and exciting. We had two different kinds of tops: one was a "beuktol," and the other was a "zweeptol." The Dutch word for top is "Tol." The "beuktol" was designed to hit the other tops out of a circle, which called for lots of strategy and strength. The "zweeptol" was a top that you got started on the sidewalk or street, and then you had a stick with a string attached to it with which you kept hitting the "zweeptol" to keep it going. The object was to keep the "zweeptol" going as long as you could. Once you got the hang of it you could go on walks with it, to see how far you could get it to follow you along going up and down over curbs. I must say, I was good at that because I could devote lots of time practicing.

Another thing I was particularly good at was jumping rope and I would do that for hours. There were lots of games you could do with the jump rope all by yourself, but it was more fun to jump rope with others. Sometimes we had two jump ropes, and we would have two people stand across from each other turning each rope in the opposite direction. You then had to jump into the ropes and zigzag to avoid getting caught in the rope. That was lots of fun as well, but very hard to master at first. Once you got the hang of it you could do it for a long time and when we got even better, we could have three or four kids jump together, depending on the size of the jump ropes. Another thing I often did with the jump ropes was moving the rope under me twice before I would hit the ground again. That wasn't all that easy! I would see if I could do it long enough so I could recite the entire alphabet. Each time you jumped you said a letter of the alphabet until you got to "Z."

We all shared whatever things we had to entertain us. I remember one kid had a set of stilts. I learned to walk with those and that was so much fun because I could see so much farther away, which allowed me to see the world from a different perspective. I would dream that I was that tall and could see that much all the time.

When I was a little older, I learned to roller skate, which brought more challenges. I had to roller skate on sidewalks which were not smooth like here in America. And there were no parking lots to practice on. But never mind that, I did what *we* could with what *we* had and had a great time anyway even though I fell down a lot to begin with and walked with big, thick scabs on my knees that whole summer. Every time a crust formed, I would fall down again, and the healing process had to start all over. Eventually I became very good at roller skating and could do all kinds of things on them. I am surprised that I never broke a knee, or that I don't have any knee problems thus far.

I feel sorry for kids in today's world. They mostly sit inside and watch TV or sit behind their computers and play games. Playing outside gave me lots of exercise, taught me several skills, and most of all, got me out of the house without getting me into trouble. One of my friends had a bicycle she let me use once in a while. It was very nice that she did as I didn't know how to ride it yet and I fell down a lot. There were no such things as training wheels then, and one learned by falling and getting up over and over again. Once I could ride a bicycle and my mom had a little extra money, I could rent a bike every so often for one hour. I had to walk to the bicycle rental place and check one out and then bring it back within the hour or get charged for another hour. I felt so rich that I had a bicycle all for myself for one whole hour even though it was for such a short time.

During the week while my brothers, sister, and I were in school there was no time for outside play. We would come home from school and my mother would be waiting for us with a cup of tea and sometimes a cookie. We talked a little about how school went, always keeping in mind that we didn't want to get yelled at or beaten, so we never volunteered any more than we absolutely had to. We also tried to make everything sound better than it was. So, conversations about my day at school, or anything else for that matter, were rather superficial. I never felt that I could bring up anything that had happened that was out of the ordinary, good or bad. After we had our tea, we had to do our homework. I remember that very well as I always ended up being very upset. I had to make sure that whatever I wrote down with my pencil was the correct answer, as my mother became very displeased if I had to erase. She didn't like the mess that was made by erasing; I had to carefully pick up every crumb. If she so happened to look the other way, I would quickly sweep it onto the floor.

Making friends and building relationships was very hard. I could not have any of my classmates or kids I had befriended in the neighborhood visit me, nor could I visit them because of a concept called "obligation." If I went to someone's house and they invited me over for lunch or even a snack, then my parents would have to reciprocate in a very similar manner. Since our lifestyle and resources were very meager, my parents were very embarrassed to have my friends come over. They just didn't have enough money to reciprocate properly. So eventually, they wouldn't let us have any friends visit. Unfortunately, you can't keep kids from talking and relating to other kids, so we would meet each other on the way to school. We talked about the things they had been doing, where they had gone over the weekend or during their vacations. Their lives were so much more exciting than mine, but I kept on listening and dreaming of the day that I could visit those places and do the things they had done. They talked about visits with relatives and what games they had learned. Of course, I wanted to learn them too and usually I didn't have too much trouble catching up with them. One thing I was never really was good at was running.

When I was about ten or twelve, we were invited by a good friend of my parents to take baths at her apartment since we still didn't have any bathtub or shower at home, and she knew how much we liked sitting and splashing in the water. It was a real treat for us as she had one of those big, deep soaking tubs. Once a week on Wednesday afternoon we would walk over to her house after school and walk home once we were done bathing. My mom's friend lived about two or three miles away from us, but we didn't care. We got out of school early on Wednesdays and were thrilled to be able to do something different. One Wednesday afternoon I was walking with eight or ten other girls who lived in the neighborhood where my "aunt" lived. I don't remember my younger sister or brother being with me. I think I went alone that day. Anyway, I really did not know these girls very well as I only saw them on those walks to my aunt's house. One of them decided to go "belletje trekken" which means that you ring someone's doorbell and then run away as fast as you can. We had done it before in that same street and always got away with it, so we weren't too worried about what might happen. Well, this time someone started running after us and everyone took off in different directions. Nobody paid attention as to who of us fell behind or not, and sure enough, I got caught.

I was the slowest person running away, and then suddenly, I felt someone grab a hold of me. This big guy then dragged me home with him and as expected, none of the other girls came to my rescue. We had to walk about a half a block which seemed like forever. I was crying and begging to be set free, but he was going to teach me a lesson, he said. Finally, we reached his house, and he took me to the cellar which was very dark and not very deep. It was probably more a crawlspace than anything else. He pushed me inside, closed the door and yelled something to the effect that I might never get out of there. I had never been so scared in my life. I cried like crazy and wet my pants. After a while his wife came and rescued me. She urged me to leave quickly, but not before I promised her that I would never do it again or worse things would happen to me. She didn't have to worry about that — I had certainly learned my lesson.

I arrived at my aunt's house later than expected, and she asked why I was so late. Somehow, I was able to hide the fact that I had just experienced something terrifying and that I had wet my pants. I just told her that I had played with some other kids and had forgotten about the time. I didn't dare tell her what had really happened for fear she would tell my parents and I would receive more punishment for being involved in such a horrible thing. Looking back, I don't think she would have told them. Of course, I didn't tell my parents either.

When my mom or dad's friends or relatives visited our house, we kids weren't allowed to stay in the living room very long. We had to greet the guests, politely ask them how they were doing, and give them a kiss on each cheek. Then we had to leave and play very quietly in our room until they left, at which time we had to come out of our room to tell them goodbye and kiss them again. There was never a choice about giving the kisses, or at least we didn't think so. We just knew we were expected to do so. Usually that wasn't a problem, but there was one friend of my parents who often smelled bad. We really didn't want to come too close to her, let alone kiss her. She was a very nice lady who would have given you the shirt off her back, but she had asthma really bad. In order for her to stop wheezing she smoked horrible smelling cigarettes that were supposed to open her bronchial tubes. They smelled like menthol, and she smelled like menthol as well. To this day I hate the smell of menthol. She always came by bike, and later by moped. In the winter she wore several coats and sweaters to keep warm and dry. When she took off all those extra layers of clothing, she smelled rather sweaty. Between the scent of sweat and the menthol cigarettes, she smelled pretty horrible. We weren't too keen on giving her a kiss, especially in the winter. But like good little kids, we did what our parents asked us to do.

During most of my school years I was teased a lot by my schoolmates. Kids know who is an easy target, and it must have been written all over my forehead. Besides being teased about the hand-me-downs we got from the Salvation Army; I got teased a lot about many other things as well. It seemed like no day went by that they couldn't find something that they could pick on me for. The way I wore my hair, the way I talked and related to kids (remember, I couldn't talk about similar experiences), the time of night I had to go to bed. I remember having to go to bed at 7:00 pm every day until I was about 12 years old. On Friday and Saturday night and during vacations I could stay up until 7:30 p.m. What a deal! None of the other kids had to go to bed that early, and I often wondered why I had to. Other than not being able to play with other kids, I didn't mind going to bed so early, at least not in the summer, or when it was light enough to do some reading. I loved reading, and by having to go to bed so early gave me extra time to read my books. My sister and I slept in bunk beds; I had the top bunk. I would keep the curtain open a crack and lay with my book as close to the window as possible and get a couple of hours reading in before going to sleep. I remember reading a book a day in those days. To get books, I had to walk to the "library," which was in the back of a little store on the street where we used to live with my aunt. People had to pay a dime for each book they borrowed. This was a lot of money for us; something we could not really afford. The store was owned and run by a couple who knew us well. When the lady was running the store, she would let me have the books for free, which saved my mom and dad quite a bit of money and giving me the pleasure of getting as many books to read as possible.

When I got sleepy, I would crawl all the way under the covers and put my head at the end of the bed and my feet under my pillow so I would be safe. I don't know what I was afraid of, but I somehow felt safer and slept better if my head was not visible. My mom would wake me up before she went to bed and make me go to the bathroom one more time hoping I would make it through the night without wetting the bed. (I was still wetting the bed when I was nine or ten.) She would have a difficult time getting me out of bed and was worried that I wouldn't get enough air sleeping that way. She made sure that I was back in bed the normal way, but as soon as she was gone, I put my head way down under the covers again. I wanted to feel safe so badly.

Every fall, when the stores would get ready for Sinterklaas (St. Nick), I would be especially well behaved because I still believed in Sinterklaas. This was another reason for kids to tease me. They had figured out long ago that he was just someone who dressed up as Sinterklaas. Even though I had my doubts, I still believed in the good old man until I was about 11 years old. I wanted so badly to believe that there was someone who would see the good in me and treat me special. I didn't feel like there were too many positive things going on for me at the time, so if there was a Sinterklaas who treated little kids with kindness, I wanted desperately to believe in him.

On the fifth of December we would always hear a knock on the front door, and somebody had to go down to open the door. I was never brave enough to go down because I didn't know what might happen. What if I hadn't been good enough and "Zwarte piet," his black helper, would put me in the big bag he carried over his shoulder and take me away to Spain? So, my older brother would go down and come back with a basket full of presents. More anxiety arose because maybe I wouldn't get any presents or just some pieces of coal. Of course, that didn't happen. However, I quickly noticed that each year we would get the same presents. Since we didn't have much money, there would always be things we would need; new slippers, an item of clothing, a box of colored pencils, and the thing I liked the best — a jar of the really good jam. I would have a whole jar for myself and could eat it whenever I wanted. Wow!!! I didn't care too much for the other presents as they were always something I really didn't want, or I had to take really good care of. The slippers were the kind that would keep your feet warm but were in drab colors, nothing cute for girls. The pencils were very nice, but I had to be careful that I didn't break them while coloring and wear them out too fast. We didn't get coloring books as my mother wanted us to draw pictures ourselves. I wasn't good at that at all so it wasn't much fun to have nice coloring pencils. The only thing I could draw nicely was abstract figures. Then there was the issue of my choosing color combinations. I liked green and blue which clashed according to my parents. I didn't understand why as those colors are seen in nature a lot. And I liked purples and yellows. Again, not good. I had to basically draw what they wanted me to draw, and once again I had to be very careful that I didn't have to erase.

CHAPTER 6

My teen years weren't much better. I was still receiving conflicting messages that confused me tremendously. I still couldn't participate in any after school activities, but I did have to help with the variety of chores my mother gave us to do. I still wasn't told why I could do the chores but couldn't do other afternoon activities. Now I know that the real reason was lack of money.

Activities cost money and there still wasn't any extra money to spend. Every month my mother had to be able to account for every penny spent, right down to the last one. If she couldn't, she and my dad argued and argued, and my mother ended up crying. Sometimes she was just a little off, maybe ten or fifteen cents.

When I started Junior High School, I had to walk to school at least a couple of miles while carrying my school bag. There were no school buses and public transportation was not in the budget. I lived too far away from home to be able to go home for lunch, and often had six or eight classes a day. My school bags were extremely heavy since everything I needed for the whole day was in there. My bag must have weighed at least 10 pounds because of all the books, gym clothes, and shoes. On the day that I had geography class, I had to carry a big atlas while at other times I might have to carry a dictionary. On gym day I had to bring my gym clothes and tennis shoes. My parents wouldn't allow me to wear tennis shoes to school because it was thought that they weren't good for your feet when walking long distances or wearing them all day long. It was okay to have them on for the hour during gym class, but absolutely no longer than that. My parents believed my weak feet needed all the help they could get. How I envied my classmates who could wear their gym shoes to school and therefore didn't have to carry them in their bag.

There was a girl in one of my classes who was also not very popular because of two things. First, she was extremely smart, which often is a threat to the other kids, and second, she was physically handicapped because of a birth defect. Her left arm and hand were okay, but her right arm stopped just below the elbow, and she had a little hand that was at a 45-degree angle towards her body. She had a bicycle and rode by my house every day. She saw me walking to school every day. One day she said that I could put my school bag on the back seat of her bike, and we would walk to school together. It was so nice, since I didn't have to do the long walk by myself, and I didn't have to carry my heavy school bag. After doing this for a few days she suggested that we might as well ride together on her bike. She would sit on the seat, start riding, and I would hold both our school bags while running next to her and then jump on the rear bike rack. At first it was quite a trick and she swayed in and out of traffic on the busiest street in town. But soon she became quite good at it, and I was able to jump on the back without too much trouble.

One day my dad was sick and stayed home from work. He looked out the window as I was leaving for school and saw me jumping on her bike as I balanced both of our school bags. When I came home from school, he immediately wanted to know who she was and told me to bring her over to the house. He wasn't very thrilled about me doing this dangerous thing to begin with. You should have seen his face when he met her and found out that she only had one arm.

I had to promise not to do it ever again, and he, in turn, promised me that he would buy me a bike of my own as soon as he had saved up the money for one. I told him that would be great, but I went one step further and asked if, in the meantime, I could roller skate to school to help me get there faster. He agreed, so when the weather was good, I skated to school. I was good on my skates and could do all kinds of tricks. Skating to school gave me time to improve my skating abilities even more and got me to school less tired. On the other hand, I had to carry the skates with me all day long. We didn't have lockers in school, and I had to carry everything needed for that day with me. Sometimes it wasn't easy lugging around my skates all day long, but it was worth it to me.

Luckily it wasn't too long before I had a new bike of my own which I parked in the parking garage under the school. The parking garage was for bicycles only. During the 1950s very few teachers, and certainly no students owned cars. One had to be at least eighteen years old to get a driver's license, and cars were very expensive.

My father spent quite a bit of money on the bike because he wanted to make sure that I got the safest one possible. My bike had drum brakes because the salesperson said that they were the best brakes to have in a rainy country. The caliper type brakes with rubber pads wouldn't do the job in the rain as they could slip and not stop the bike in time. The new bike was a blessing, but also a big worry. To this day I remember how proud I was riding around on my new bike. The sun was shining and everything on my bike that wasn't painted was sparkling in the sun. I was so proud and happy and felt so rich. This was the first really nice thing I had ever received in my whole life, and it was mine. As I was riding around in a side street looking at all the different shiny parts of my bike and admiring all the shiny spokes, I wasn't paying attention to where I was going. The next thing I know I was laying on the ground with my bike next to me. I had run into a parked car. Fortunately for me, there was no damage to the car. I had a few scratches on my knee and elbow which was no big deal as that happened almost daily. I was always falling or running into things because I didn't pay attention like I should. My new bike now had some scratches on it, and I knew what would happen if my father found out. I tried to hide it from him as long as I could, but eventually he found out. Of course, he wanted to know how it had happened, and I had to tell him something. I don't remember exactly what I told him. It wouldn't really have made any difference as I got punished anyway. He wanted me to keep that bike in tip-top shape.

Every week I had to wash it and every so often I had to wax it too. The wax would prevent the bike from rusting. Cars and bikes rust easily when you live close to the seacoast, and you don't even have to be that close. This was a big job, and one I didn't like at all. Washing and waxing my bike took time away from me riding around and exploring parts of the town I hadn't seen yet. Can you imagine washing every spoke, then thoroughly drying it before waxing every spoke? Even worse than doing all the spokes was cleaning and waxing the drum brakes. It was hard to reach them through the spokes no matter how small my fingers were and every single inch had to be cleaned and polished to prevent rust from getting on the drum brakes.

In the summertime I used some light wax — the kind that goes on easily and is removed easily. But in the winter, when there was a lot of damp weather, I had to use a thick, paste-type wax. I remember that it looked kind of like petroleum jelly. I'm sure I took some shortcuts doing that job and eventually little patches of rust showed up here and there. Once that happened, we had to try to remove it, but in the long run it was a lost cause. I kept that bike until I moved to Germany, after I was married, at which time I either gave it away to a friend or sold it very cheaply. I don't remember which now.

I had to take dance lessons. Once a week, on Saturday, I was sent off to one of the most reputable dancing schools in town. The reason I had to learn to dance was that it was considered part of growing up and one needed to have a well-rounded and balanced upbringing. I really looked forward to this new experience but unless the teacher paired me up with someone, I ended up being a wallflower most of the time. There were more girls than boys signed up and with my self-esteem being as low as it was, I wasn't very outgoing or talkative. Nobody believes it now when I say that I used to be shy, but it was true. So, often I would sit out most of the dances. Of course, this didn't make me a good dancer. As time went on, I really didn't want to go anymore. However, it was a chance to be out of the house again, so I continued going. At one point I met a nice young man who took a liking to me and would dance with me every opportunity he had. He might have been my very first male friend — but not a boyfriend.

Unfortunately, I couldn't be with him other than at the dance because in my father's eyes he came from a "lower status" family than us. His father was a blue-collar worker, and we were white-collar people. And never the two shall mix! Anyway, I was supposed to learn to dance, and I did. For the graduation dance we had to come with a partner and be nicely dressed. My friend wanted to take me to the dance, and I was so excited and accepted right away. But first I had to clear it with my parents. So, I told them about the upcoming dance and that this boy had asked me to be his partner. My father told me that he had to ask his permission officially by mail, since there was no telephone in our house. Nobody did that anymore; it was old-fashioned and unheard of, even then. My father wouldn't budge so I had to go and tell my friend about it. He said he would be glad to and promptly mailed the needed letter. I thought everything was fine until my dad told me that the invitation hadn't been written properly and that it was obvious that he wasn't our kind of people. I don't remember if I got to go or not. I seem to have memory lapses about certain things in my life. Anyway, the message again was very clear. I had to learn certain things in life but couldn't count on using them always because of prejudice. Even though we were poor, I was supposed to mingle with higher-society people, but they wouldn't come to our house because we didn't meet their expectations. How could I win in a situation like that?

My first year in High School was uneventful, but I did pass into the next grade. In the Netherlands I took 12 or 13 subjects each year and the classes were taught like college classes here. I had five or six class periods every day but never the same classes each day. If we had three subjects or more with grades of five or less (on a scale of one to

ten with ten being the highest grade) you had to repeat the whole year
— all the classes.

The next year I had additional math and science and flunked. In
fact, in one of my math classes I retook a test which I knew I had
flunked. I figured that if the teacher didn't see it, I wouldn't have a bad
mark for that test. I didn't hand the test in and when he gave back all
the tests, he asked why mine wasn't there. I said that I didn't understand why he didn't have my test as I had handed it in and he must
have lost it. I'm sure he knew what had happened and tried to argue
his point. I stood my ground, and he couldn't do anything other than
to give me the benefit of the doubt. He told me that I had to retake
the test the following day. I sure hadn't counted on that! I needed to
have more time to study. So, the next day I didn't show up for the test
which was after the regular scheduled classes. I hadn't figured out how
to tell my mother that I had to stay after school, so I just went home.
I finally did take the test and I'm sure I didn't do much better than
before. Math just wasn't my cup of tea. Anyway, I flunked that year,
so my parents had some choices to make. Would I do this year over or
take the track where the emphasis would be more on languages?

My parents decided to switch me to the language track, which
meant that besides the regular classes like history, geography, art, a
lower-level math, etc., I now had six language classes. In addition to
Dutch, German, French, and English, I also had Greek and Latin. So,
one day I might go from German to Greek and then to French while
the next day I might have Dutch, German, and Latin. Surprisingly,
that wasn't too much of a problem for me. I liked languages and they
made much more sense than trying to figure out how much water you
have to take out of a full container to put a brick in it and not have
it overflow. Languages to me had a purpose, and I wanted to learn
all about them. Who cares about a stupid brick and the water tank?
When was I going to need to know that anyway? I felt the same about
algebra. When would I use more than adding, subtracting, multiply-
ing, or dividing? I did enjoy learning to figure out the roots of numbers

and would spend hours doing that when I had nothing else to do. But languages were a different story. If I ever got to go to visit all the wonderful countries I had read and learned about, I wanted to be able to speak the language of the people who lived there.

Sadly, I didn't do too well in three of the classes and I flunked again. I remember to this day my mother's reaction when my report card came in the mail. I could have intercepted the card, and I might have hidden it for a couple of days. But not for very long, as my parents knew approximately when the card would arrive in the mail. All I would have gained was a mere day or two. I went down to get the mail and showed my mom the report card. I swear she looked green when she saw that I had flunked again. I hadn't seen her that frightened before and I knew that I was in deep trouble once my dad came home. I must have suppressed that memory because I don't remember now what happened when he saw the report card. Obviously, I was done with the options at that school unless I was willing to retake the second year over again. This would mean that I would be 16 and the other students in the class 12 and 13 years old.

After long deliberation the decision was made, and I was told that it was time to switch me to another school, the M.M.S or "Middlebare Meisjes School" — an all-girl high school where the classes were taught at a somewhat lower level than the school I had attended before. The previous school had been for students who were going to be doctors, lawyers, etc. The diploma from the M.M.S. wasn't going to get me into a university, but I would certainly be able to get a good job after graduation. And even after finishing the third year in that school I would stand a decent chance in the job market. Official graduation came after the fifth year and passing all the tests given.

This was the first year I had some real friends, and this made going to school much more bearable. There were four of us who always ran around together, and we were called the four musketeers. My father was doing a little better financially and I could have friends over once in a while. I still went to friends' houses much more than they came to my house. I felt so much more at ease away from home.

I did have to decide as to what I was going to do once I was done with the school year. I knew that I didn't want to go to school any longer and that I wanted to have a job and be on my own — live in my own apartment, make my own decisions and become independent. However, I was too young to be on my own yet even if I had a job.

I had read about Florence Nightingale and always thought that caring for sick people was a very rewarding thing to do. If I finished the year, I would still only be 16, going on 17, but I needed to be eighteen before I could start a nursing program. So, I needed to do something for another year. I didn't see any point in studying another year at this school I was in if I wasn't going to finish the five-year program anyway. There was no point in taking some other kind of job for a year and then quitting that. So, I decided to go to the "Huishoudschool." This was a school where you learned how to take care of a family, how to cook, wash clothes and iron them, sew and clean, and to take care of children. After finishing the program, one could become a nanny or a good housekeeper. I think it was excellent training in preparation for motherhood especially in the 1960s when mothers stayed home once there was a baby in the house. I liked most of what I learned there except that you had to learn to use equipment that might be available in a hypothetical house, but as a rule would be outdated. For example, we had to learn to iron with non-electric flat irons. We had to heat them on a stove, use them until they were too cold to get the wrinkles out, and then switch to the other one that had been heating while we were ironing. Even my mother had an electric iron and a few women even had irons with thermostats in them.

The school's philosophy was that you could be working for some-one out in the country who still used outdated equipment. Another thing we had to learn was to wash our clothes in a kettle with water — nothing new to me as my mother had always done that. However, we couldn't use the detergent that you buy in the store, the kind that came in nice boxes with little measuring scoops inside them. We had to take a bar of soap, put it in a strainer and slosh it through the water, back and forth, back and forth, until there were enough suds to wash clothes. By the time we had enough suds the water was barely warm. Learning to use an electric sewing machine was the most worrisome experience of all. This was a new adventure for most of us students. I didn't know anyone in my class who had ever seen one in use. Before we could even come close to the machine, we were told that these machines were very fast and almost uncontrollable and that it was very easy to get hurt on them. In other words, they were very dangerous. And sure enough, the first time one girl used it she had her finger too close to the foot and the needle went right through her finger. There was no way I was going to use that machine since I believed she was smarter than I was and that if she got hurt on it I certainly would too. I don't think I tried to use that machine during that year and always volunteered for the old-fashioned ones that you either turned by hand or by foot treadle. In fact, my very first sewing machine I got after I was married was with a foot treadle. It would be an antique now and I wish I still had it.

My favorite class was cooking because we got to eat the things we prepared after the class was over. Making cakes was the absolute best and I always ended up with too little frosting or whipping cream. I ate most of it before I got it on the cake. Needless to say, I gained some weight that year, but that was all right, as I was still rather skinny when I started school.

The teen years continued to be very confusing for me. I really didn't have anyone to talk to until I was seventeen or eighteen about what was going on inside me and what to expect and not to expect. The only thing I remember is that I was told that I should watch out for boys because they only wanted one thing from girls and it always meant that you would have a baby. I was never told what the boys really wanted or about how babies were brought into this world. I was so scared that just kissing a boy would make me pregnant that I didn't even look at a boy for fear that would happen to me. My father would have killed me. Not really, but life would have been hell for sure.

I remember having terrible crushes on certain movie stars. I bought any magazine that had photographs of them in it and pasted all the pictures neatly in a scrapbook. Every day I would look in the book and daydream what life would be like if I was either one of them or if I was married to one of them. I also daydreamed of being married to a prince and eventually we would be the king and queen. All these people seemed to have such wonderful lives and had everything they could possibly want. They were treated very special and loved by everybody around them (again my perception as I later learned that they are often the loneliest people in the world). They lived in beautiful homes and castles with maids and servants but most of all they were warm, had bathtubs and showers, and ate the kinds of foods they wanted whenever they wanted.

I went to sleep praying and hoping that I would wake up with a solution for getting out of the lonely, poor situation I was in. How much I wanted to be loved and accepted, to be warm and not hungry, to have the things that the other kids in my class had and most of all be accepted for who I was.

My first crush was a bit closer to reality. He was one of my teachers, not a movie star or prince — just a regular person. I was only thirteen or fourteen years old. He rode a bike to school and so did I. I would wait for him after school and then ride my bike next to him as far as we were going in the same direction. It either took him awhile to catch on to what was going on, or he didn't know how to handle the situation. Finally, he told me what he thought was happening and explained gently, but firmly, that this couldn't go on. I was heartbroken, of course, but got over it.

My next "love" was a house painter who thought that I was eighteen. He would take me to the beach in his car and bring soda pop along and throw away the empty bottles. I was raised that every bottle is worth money because of the deposit refund when you returned it to the store. I was impressed that he could afford to buy soda pop whenever he wanted and could afford to throw away the bottles, but at the same time it bothered me that he didn't take them back to the store, and that he cluttered up the streets with the bottles.

We went on long walks together on the beach. If the weather was nice, we would take off our shoes and socks and walk through the water. When we got tired of walking, we sat down to rest for a while and do some smooching in the dunes behind the beach. However, it was nothing serious. He tried to do more, but I kept resisting. I was too worried what might happen and what my father would do to us if he found out. When he learned that I was only fourteen he broke off with me because he didn't want to wait for seven more years to get married. A girl had to be twenty-one to be able to get married at that time. Soon after that I started gaining some weight, and I never had many more experiences with boys until I was eighteen or nineteen. Besides, it was hard for me to go on dates when I had to be home by eight o'clock.

I was feeling even lonelier than ever and would have joined a harem in Morocco if someone had asked me. I had only read about the more glamorous parts of life in a harem. I was ready to settle for sharing love and attention with other girls, wearing beautiful dresses, living in a warm climate, and eating delicious food. I never heard about the kind of things I would have had to do in return for living such a life. All I wanted was to be loved by someone. Fortunately for me, I found out what life in a harem was really like when I was watching a movie one day. I don't remember the title of the movie, but the scenes were very explicit and scary enough for me to change my mind about living like that. However, I never stopped daydreaming about faraway places, big, beautiful houses, trips to romantic islands, or just being somewhere better than where I was now. Subconsciously I was setting my mind to figure out how I could leave the Netherlands and go to a place where everything was bigger and better.

CHAPTER 7

Towards the end of my year at the Huishoudschool, my mom started taking me to different hospitals to find out which one would accept me in their nursing program. I was excited as this meant that I could soon be on my own. There was hope now; that my chains would soon be broken. I found out that I would get room and board and even some spending money, if accepted, and I would be truly independent of my parents. Although I still had doubts that I could become a nurse given that my father wasn't supportive of me becoming a nurse. He thought nursing was a demeaning job; putting people on bedpans and taking care of personal needs they might have. He thought a nurse was socially only one step higher than a maid. He had much higher expectations for his daughter. I don't know why he thought that since I had been given the impression that I wasn't the smartest kid on the block and my past record proved it. At any rate, I knew that there was more to nursing than bedpans and cleaning people up after they made a mess. I wanted passionately to help people feel better while they were in pain or sick. I knew how it felt to be in pain or ill and felt that I could relate to them. My mother was very supportive of my ambitions as she had been a nurse herself and her father had been a doctor.

So, in the spring of 1960 she took me to all the local hospitals to see if I could enter a nursing program that fall. At each hospital, she came along to talk to the person in charge of hiring. She was worried about my abilities to take the training to become a nurse. She shared her concerns with the person who interviewed us and made sure they knew that I wasn't very smart. She said that right in front of me at each hospital. And each time, although the hospital didn't really reject me, they suggested that I try the program at the Rode Kruis Ziekenhuis, which translates literally as the Red Cross Hospital. However, the hospital was not connected with the worldwide Red Cross organization. It just happened to use the same name for its building.

All the hospitals were in the downtown area and were old and dilapidated. The Rode Kruis Ziekenhuis, however, was building a new hospital not too far from where I lived. It was going to be the most modern facility in the area and maybe even in all of the Netherlands. To my surprise, I was accepted at the Rode Kruis Ziekenhuis and was to start training in October once the hospital was finished. I really didn't want to wait any longer than necessary; I wanted to gain my independence and be out of the house. When I asked if there was a way I could start sooner, I was in luck. They told me I was able to start in August because they needed people to help with cleaning the new hospital before it could be used. I was so excited! I would be on my own sooner than expected. My wish had been granted. I could hardly wait and counted the days, already making plans about what I would do first and how I would spend my free time.

My life was now going to be the way I wanted it to be. Now I would be much more in control of my own life. I might even start dreaming again. But I was thinking, when I finally moved into my little room at the hospital, after all I had gone through and all the disappointments I had experienced in my life, did I dare dream one more time? My thoughts were so contradictory. It would be wonderful if I could dream once again and if at least some of it came true. I could hardly imagine what that would feel like. But then I thought about the effect it would have on me if I dared to dream once more and the dream again didn't come true. Would I be able to take another disappointment? These thoughts and the feelings that went with them were confusing and frightening. I did not think that my dreams were so special, but somehow, they never seemed to come true for me.

Sure, I dreamed of exotic trips to faraway places, of living in a roomy beautiful house with a swimming pool and a spacious yard around it. But I knew that those thoughts and dreams were the kind that every teenager has and eventually outgrow them — especially since they realize that very few people ever have their dreams come true. What I really hoped for was to be loved for who I am and be told that I did a good job and was a capable person. I didn't think that this was such a crazy dream, but at home in the Netherlands, it never happened. Would I ever be able to find somebody to take care of me, to support me and to think I wasn't so stupid after all? Would my knight in shining armor ever show up on my doorstep? What could he ever see in someone like me? And if he did show up and sweep me off my feet, did I really want to be taken care of and have no control over my life? I didn't really know anymore; all I knew is that I wanted something different than what I had now. I had my doubts, but I kept on hoping and dreaming.

In the meantime, my parents decided to cancel the health insurance they had on me at the end of June thinking that nothing major would happen until I started work. After all, other than colds and sinus infections, I really hadn't had anything wrong with me for years. However, a week or so after they canceled the insurance, I had my first appendicitis attack. I still remember that day. I had been invited by one of my friend's parents to spend a week in Lunteren, a quiet little town in the Veluwe in the eastern part of the Netherlands. I joyfully accepted, but at the same time I was a bit surprised that my parents allowed me to go as this would entail obligations on our part again.

My friend and I rode our bicycles from Den Haag to Utrecht, where we would catch the train to Arnhem (the bikes were put on the train as well) and from Arnhem we rode to Lunteren. It was a whole day affair, but we were excited. The weather cooperated making the entire journey very pleasant. A couple of days after we got there, I had sharp pains in the lower right side of my body. My friend's sister, who was a nurse, thought it could be an appendicitis attack. I lay down for a while and the pain subsided. I couldn't go to the doctor to have it checked out because I didn't have insurance, and I surely didn't have any money to pay a doctor. However, I figured that I would be taken care of in a few weeks by one of the doctors at the hospital. This was not to be and turned out to be the beginning of attacks, severe pain, being nauseated, and trouble for the next three years. All the while I was working in the hospital, I continued to have attacks but received countless excuses about my pains.

Appendicitis was very hard to diagnose then. I was even tested for gallbladder problems because by then I was very much overweight, and they thought that my problems stemmed from that. When I started working in the hospital, I was not fat, but it only took me less than 2 months to gain forty pounds or so. I was rather chubby by then. It was also thought that I was faking the symptoms because I wanted to have some time off. In those days one stayed in the hospital for a week after an appendectomy. Then you had to recuperate a couple of weeks before going back to work. So, you were out of commission for a minimum of three weeks while continuing to draw your full wages.

I had my first experience with HMOs long before they became popular in America. So, I walked around with appendicitis attacks for three years because I wasn't allowed to change doctors. It was a very ironic situation. Here I was working in a hospital where some of the finest doctors treated all kinds of people and I, one of their nurses, couldn't get the care I so desperately needed because they didn't want to believe I had problems with my appendix. I learned again that asking for help doesn't necessarily produce results. Much later in life I learned that there were people who could and would actually help you.

Finally, my mother was able to persuade her doctor, who also had operated on my sister's appendix, to check me over. One day, quite unexpectedly, I was summoned to his office so he could examine me. Naturally, I didn't have any problems that day, but I was able to tell him where I had been hurting and how I had been feeling for the past three years. He told me that he was sure that my appendix needed to be taken out. A week later I was operated on my appendix. I would have been operated sooner, but I had a boil on my left hand and the surgeon wanted to wait until that was gone.

I was very glad to have my appendix removed because I would feel so much better afterwards. At the same time, I became very concerned at what might happen if they operated on me and couldn't find any problems with my appendix. After all, they had been telling me all this time that the symptoms were all in my head and there was nothing wrong with me. What if they had been right and I had been wrong all this time? This big nagging doubt came over me again. As soon as I woke up from the surgery and knew what was going on I asked the doctor what he had found. He assured me that it was good thing that my appendix was removed because it was nothing but scar tissue and that I was lucky to be alive. Apparently, all these attacks that supposedly had been in my head had been real attacks and could eventually have killed me. If my appendix had burst, I could have died. I reminded him again that I had been walking around for three years with symptoms and that nobody had believed me. He wasn't too happy to hear that.

Convinced that I hadn't faked the whole thing I enjoyed the rest and care given to me. My mother and sister came to visit me soon after I was back in my room. I was still groggy, but my sense of humor was already awake. I told my mother in a very sleepy voice that I had lost something. She wanted to make sure that she could help me find it and asked what I had lost. I again told her groggily, "I lost something." She asked again what I had lost and said she would help me find it. I told her that she couldn't ever find it back because I had really lost it. She finally insisted that I tell her what I had lost. I told her that I had lost my appendix. Everybody had a big laugh, including me, but I soon found out that it hurt way too much to laugh, so I didn't tell any more jokes for a few days after that. After a week my stitches were removed, and I was released from the hospital. I did my recuperation at my boyfriend's house. His mom and dad had invited me to spend some time with them, and during the weekends I could visit with him when he was home on leave. My mom and dad had offered the same, but I didn't want to go back home. I rather would have spent time in my own apartment. Anyway, it was nice to catch up on my rest as the last months had been very tiring. Two weeks later my doctor decided, after a thorough examination, that I wasn't ready to go back to work. He told me to take another two weeks off. I didn't argue about that one bit as I still tired easily and enjoyed the following weeks, making sure I came to work only to collect my pay. We were paid once a month. We all stood in line and were handed a little envelope with cash in it, right down to the last penny. I always felt so rich having money in my hand and had to get used to getting paid by check later in life.

The nursing program at the Rode Kruis Ziekenhuis ended up being the best experience I could have had. It provided me with lots of on-the-job training, much more than I would have received at any of the other hospitals where most of the time was spent in classrooms. What a wonderful feeling it was to be enrolled in the nursing program! Even though I hadn't officially started in the nursing program I was very proud to wear the uniform of the hospital and to be part of it from the start. We scrubbed and cleaned and made everything look fantastic. In October of 1960 the official opening of the hospital took place with the Dutch Queen Juliana present and making the rounds. That was the closest I ever was to the queen, just an arm's length away. She sure didn't look like anyone special. She looked like a regular person, which of course she was. She just had been lucky enough to be born into a royal family.

The wing for the nurses' rooms was connected to the hospital and made it very easy to go to work. I didn't even have to go outside to go to work. I finally had a room of my own. I could decorate it however I wanted to and didn't have to share it with anyone. The room was no bigger than a good-sized walk-in closet. However, I didn't care. I was happy as a lark at being able to come and go, play music when I wanted, and listen to what I wanted. I could stay up as late as I wanted and, on my days, off, I could sleep as late as I wanted. I could lay on the bed whenever I wanted and put my feet on the bed when I sat in my chair. All those things I hadn't been allowed to do while living at home. There was a small sink in the corner of the room, but the toilet and showers were down the hall and shared with many others. I still felt so rich because the only way I had been able to take a bath or a shower up to now was by traveling to the bathhouse or to my aunt's house. Both were a long walk away and not easily accessible. Now, I only had to walk a few steps and could take a nice, warm shower for as long as I wanted. And I sure made use of that. I still enjoy long, hot showers. I got three excellent meals a day and oftentimes a snack in between. My uniforms got washed and ironed for free and the rest of my clothes I washed in the sink, or I went to the Laundromat.

Washing clothes at the Laundromat was an experience in itself. You brought your clothes in a pillowcase or wrapped inside something big. I don't remember having laundry baskets. You handed the bundle to the lady in charge of the Laundromat who would weigh your clothes and make sure that each pile of clothing weighed no more than five kilos or eleven pounds. The whole process took a long time because the machines filled with cold water and each load had to be heated for each wash cycle. The advantage was that you could set many different water temperatures for your laundry. However, I think that it really doesn't make any difference if the water is 100 degrees or 110 degrees.

My duties in the hospital varied and increased the longer I was there. The program took three years to finish and each year I had to complete certain tests and practical skills before I could advance to the next year. I was always very nervous when I had to have another nurse watch how I was doing certain things so that they could be marked off in my book. I always worried that I wouldn't do it right. The program combined classes with practical skills from the very first day. I remember one of the first things we learned was how to change the sheets with a patient in the bed. It seemed impossible then, especially if the patient couldn't move much, or in some cases not at all. I soon learned how easy it really was.

Two of the most unpleasant things I had to do were to give shots and to prepare a dead person for release from the hospital. I always hated shots, and still do, and wanted to do it without hurting the patients any more than necessary. We practiced on oranges and that didn't seem so bad, but it really wasn't the same as giving them to actual patients. We were taught to administer shots in the thigh because it was considered very dangerous to do it in the buttocks. If the needle hits a certain spot in the buttocks, you might paralyze the patient. The thigh was the ideal area as it usually has enough muscle and there is no place to paralyze the patient. Sometimes I had to give cancer patients morphine shots for pain and had a hard time with that. They often were so thin that they didn't have much muscle or skin left because of the advancement of their disease. If you pushed the needle in a little too far you would hit the bone.

Preparing a body for the mortuary meant closing the eyes and keeping my hands on them until they stayed closed, washing the body including the hair, emptying the bladder and the intestines, stuffing cotton into the rectal area, cutting and cleaning the nails, and making the body look presentable for the family before it went to the funeral home. Presentable meant clean and neat but no make-up was put on the faces of the deceased. When this was finished the body was taken down to the basement where there were drawers to keep it cool until someone from the funeral home came to get it.

The first time I remember doing this was with the help of an older nurse. I was barely eighteen years old and had really lived a rather sheltered life. In fact, I had never even seen a dead person except for the deaths in the camp and I was too young to remember that. We washed the front of the deceased patient and then we had to do the back. I was standing on one side of the bed and the other nurse on the other side. She turned the patient over toward me and suddenly a big burst of air came out of his lungs. She almost had another body to take care of as it nearly scared me to death. I had no idea such a thing could happen as nobody had told me that this might take place. I never really got over my distaste for this duty. In fact, on my last day in the nursing program I hid in the bathroom after a patient on my floor died. I just could not face preparing another body.

Another thing I had to get used to was bathing men when I worked on the "men's floor." I didn't want to work on that floor. I was quite embarrassed as I didn't know how to handle seeing the private parts of a man. It stirred memories that I had repressed and thought I would never recall. When I was about eleven or twelve and walking home from school, I met this young man, a friend of my older brother. At least he said he was and, gullible me, I believed him. He struck up a conversation and I was flattered that somebody would be interested in little old me. Soon he invited me up to his room because there was something he wanted to show me — something special. I became curious about what that might be. Nobody else was home and we went straight to his room. He quickly showed me some books or stamps, I don't even remember what. He then asked me to sit on his bed and soon he wanted me to touch his private parts. I was shocked as I had never even seen a naked man or the private parts of a man. I told him I wanted to leave but he wouldn't let me go until I had touched his penis and rubbed it for a while. He could see I was shocked by this experience, and he told me not to tell anybody. This was our "secret."

I wanted to go home and tell my parents about it, but I didn't think they would understand or that they would blame me and punish me. So, I didn't tell anybody. The next time I saw him he asked if I wanted to go for a ride on his motorcycle. I thought that would be safe as we wouldn't be able to do the sexual things he had wanted me to do before, and I loved getting a ride on a motorcycle. We went for a ride, and I enjoyed that part until he went into some wooded area and stopped. We got off the bike and sat on a bench in the park. Fortunately, a policeman came by and asked my friend what we were doing there. He must have seen that I wasn't happy with the situation. He told us to go home immediately, which we did. As soon as I got off the bike I ran home. I don't remember if he had any more contact with me after that. I just wanted to forget about the whole thing.

I became very uneasy when I was told to work on the men's floor. Luckily for me, my first "victim" was an old man who quickly put me at ease. I did have a hard time for a while but learned how to wash men without showing that I was nervous or embarrassed about it. After all, I kept telling myself, it was just another duty I had to perform.

I did enjoy nursing very much even though it was extremely hard work. At first, we worked forty-five hours a week which was later reduced to forty hours. Every two weeks our schedules were posted, and changes were made in the shifts and floors we worked.

The floors were divided as follows: first floor for people with illnesses seen by internal medicine and heart specialists; second floor for obstetrics/gynecology; third floor for any type of surgery. These three floors were for national health plan patients with no additional insurance and were labeled third class. There were six patients in each room on one side of the hall and the most ill people had a single room across the hall. They were transferred to the rooms with six patients as soon as they got better or down to the basement after they had died. On these floors one side was for males and the other for females. They had a dayroom on each side so males and females couldn't even meet for coffee together. They also had very limited visitation hours. The fourth floor was for patients regardless of their illness, but who had some additional insurance. This was the second class with certain advantages. There were only two people in a room, longer visitation hours, and somewhat better food. They also received better medical care meaning that they received more medical tests, and the doctors spent more time with them. The fifth floor was for first class patients who had either a large amount insurance or lots of money. It had private rooms, better food, unlimited visitation rights, and much more attention by all staff, including the doctors.

There was one nurse for eight patients on the third-class floors. This may not sound like an extreme overload, but we had no aides or orderlies. We were totally responsible for every kind of care the patients needed. If a bed was empty and a new patient arrived, we would have to bring that person from admission and get them ready for room admission. This meant that we had to either give the person a bath or make sure they could take their own bath or shower. Every day we had to make sure all the patients either had a bath or took a bath, make their beds, and administer all their medications. We did the lab tests that could be performed in the patient's room. We also prepared the patients for more complicated laboratory tests as well as for surgery and took them to the operating rooms and picked them up when the surgery was over. There were no recovery rooms in those days and the patients went straight from the operating table to their rooms. Sometimes I had as many as three surgeries and one or two people who went home, all in one day.

After a patient went home the nurse had to get that bed ready for the next patient. This meant not only just changing the sheets, but laying the mattress out on the balcony if the weather was nice and washing the rest of the bed with a disinfectant solution. The disinfectant was also used on the nightstand and anything else that the next patient would use such as the washbasin, bedpan and the rectal thermometer. The nurses were also expected to squeeze the patient's oranges or peel fruit and give that as a snack in the morning and afternoon. Meals for third-class patients were brought up in big containers to the kitchen on those floors. The nurses had to make the plates ready for all their patients, keeping in mind each person's special diet. After everything was on the trays, we took them to the patients and picked them up when they were finished eating. If a patient could not eat by himself, we would have to feed him. Mealtimes could be very hectic, indeed.

I remember a very sad time when an eighteen-year-old boy, dying of cancer, asked me why he had to die. He hadn't done anything wrong and wanted to do so many things in his life. I was only eighteen years old myself and didn't have any answer for him. All I could do was hold his hand and sit there quietly with him. I felt helpless and wished

I could comfort him more. If some elderly person died, I felt bad as well but not nearly as bad as when a young one came to the end of his life. One old man I had to take care of had most of his tongue cut out because of cancer. He couldn't talk anymore and could only communicate by writing. Even though he was an old man and had experienced a full life, I still felt bad for him but not nearly as bad as for the young man who had just started life.

We were expected to wash the windows in our spare time. One time I was working on the men's floor and for once I was all caught up with all my work. It was a little bit easier to catch up with all the chores on the men's floor because they liked to help. The women didn't help as much, and I can't blame them. They finally had a chance to be taken care of and take it easy. Anyway, I started to wash the windows in the men's rooms. I kept hoping that I would not lose my balance and fall in the bed with someone. Sure enough, I fell off the chair and right into bed with this man. I was so embarrassed, but they all laughed and since nobody was hurt, I started laughing as well.

After I lived and worked in the hospital for about a year I wanted to move out and have a room elsewhere. I had gained some freedom when I left home but was still not totally free to do what I wanted. There was a curfew of 11 p.m. which seemed okay at first. After all, at home I had to be in before that even at age eighteen. But now I wanted total freedom. Since there was a shortage of rooms for the incoming class, I was allowed to live elsewhere. Normally, you were expected to live in the hospital at least the first two years of the three-year program. I rented a small upstairs apartment with another nurse, Kathleen (not her real name), in the house of Mr. and Mrs. Freek Versteeg. They were required to rent out part of their apartment because again, according to Dutch rental allotments, it was too big for them. Even more than fifteen years after World War II had ended there was still a shortage of housing, and the government told you how much space you were entitled to.

The apartment consisted of a living room, bedroom and a small kitchen. There was no refrigerator and no hot water to wash your dishes. The Versteegs furnished the whole apartment with furniture they thought we would like. In fact, before we moved in, Mr. Versteeg asked us what kind of furniture we wanted. It was all very modern and light and just perfect for us. We shared the toilet with them but took our baths or showers at the hospital. We quickly washed our face and brushed our teeth in the little kitchen before going to work.

The Versteegs knew Kathleen and her family quite well and were happy to rent to someone they knew. Kathleen, who had found us the apartment, took the small bedroom while I slept in the living room on the couch. The Versteegs soon became very close friends of mine. In fact, they treated me like their third daughter. I babysat their two daughters and son whenever they needed someone to watch them. I never expected to get paid as I was "family" and besides that I enjoyed playing with the little kids because I could pretend to be a kid again. They often invited me for supper, a visit, or to play games. Sometimes we would all go to a movie or for a walk. I was literally one of them. I kept in close contact with them after I moved to America, visiting them when I was in the Netherlands, and e-mail frequently with their oldest daughter, Berry. Sadly, both Mr. and Mr. Versteeg have passed away.

Kathleen and I got along just fine until she met Henry (not his real name), who quickly became her steady boyfriend. One day I came home after a busy day at work and found them both in my bed. I didn't really care that they were sexually involved, but why did they have to do that in my bed? After all, she had her own private bedroom. I was quite upset about that and told them so. Henry started staying overnight and Mr. Versteeg found out about that when he met Henry sneaking out early in the morning. Kathleen was told to move out as soon as possible. In the 1960s the standards for sleeping together were quite strict. Premarital sex was frowned upon and could be used as a reason to evict a tenant. I don't think that the Versteegs really cared so much that Kathleen had allowed Henry to stay overnight as they worried about being blamed if she got pregnant. I was worried about having to find someone to share the apartment with on such a short notice. Having to pay the whole rent by myself would be very hard as it would take almost all my earnings at the hospital. But the Versteegs decided that I could keep the apartment by myself and just pay what I had been paying so far. They probably didn't want somebody they didn't know move in as we had to walk by their living room and through their kitchen to get to our apartment. Since they knew me well, they didn't have to worry about closing the living room door; it just made it a lot easier for them. Also, they didn't really need the extra money but only rented out the upstairs because they had to. I was ecstatic as I now had my own living room, bedroom, and kitchen. I felt very rich now that I finally had my own place. We have a saying in the Netherlands: "een kinder hand is gauw gevuld" which roughly translates into "it is easy to please a child."

I rented from them until they moved to Amsterdam, which was a very sad day for all of us. I really cried as I felt that they were family, and they were now going to be so far away. It really wasn't all that far but anything farther than walking or a short bicycling distance was too far for me. However, we all promised to keep in touch, and they told me that I could visit them anytime I wanted. I continued to see the Versteegs regularly after they moved to Amsterdam — first by taking the train, then bicycling, and later by hitchhiking. I had to resort to bicycling as train tickets weren't cheap. Bicycling was not bad at all since there are excellent bicycle paths across the Netherlands. But it was a 35-mile trip one-way which took me a little over three hours at that time and I really couldn't do that too easily in one day — at least not if I wanted to spend some quality time with them or do some sightseeing. It would be more feasible to ride my bicycle to Amsterdam if I could spend the night with them. Since I had an open invitation with them staying overnight was no problem. I rode my bike to visit them many times until one day I learned about hitchhiking. I had started the return trip from Amsterdam and was just outside the city limits when it started raining cats and dogs. I couldn't see myself riding my bike in the rain for another three hours or so. I quickly talked myself into letting go of my fear of hitchhiking, got off my bike and slowly raised my thumb up to the first car that came by. I really hoped that some kind soul would stop his or her car and offer to give me a ride. At the same time, I was wondering what I would do if somebody did offer me a ride. I had my bike, and I was sopping wet. Cars in those days weren't necessarily big enough to put a bicycle in it. But very soon somebody did take pity on me and stopped on the side of the road. He asked me where I was going and since he had to go in the same general area, he offered me a ride in his car. To my amazement my bike fit in the trunk and soon I made it home safe and sound. After that, I never rode my bike to Amsterdam or took the train again. I figured, why travel the hard way if I could hitchhike? It was much cheaper, much more adventurous and much faster.

Hitchhiking wasn't all that dangerous in those days. Rape and molestation rarely occurred, and murders were unheard of. If you were blonde and nicely shaped, you might have to worry more about being kidnapped and be sold to a harem in Algeria or Morocco. Since I had brown hair and was overweight (Mr. Versteeg even called me a "kamer olifant" or room elephant), I wasn't too worried about what might happen. Only once did I have a somewhat scary experience, but I handled it very well, I think.

I had bought a one-way ticket for the train to Rotterdam for a meeting at the American Consulate. I figured I had to make sure I got there on time so didn't want to hitchhike for fear I would be late. Once my appointment was done, however, I decided to hitchhike to Amsterdam to visit my friends. Soon a car stopped, and the driver offered me a ride. All went fine for a while until we came to a less populated part of the Netherlands. The man proceeded to tell me what a good time we could have together once we arrived in Amsterdam. I told him that I was engaged and therefore not interested in any good time with him or anybody else. He tried to persuade me but didn't succeed. Then he asked me if I was afraid of him. My insides were shaking so hard he must have felt my uneasiness, but I pretended not to be afraid. He continued to make his advances and I felt more and more uncomfortable. So, I told him to stop the car and let me out. He laughed, pointing outside to the farms and the little country roads, and told me that I would never get a ride to Amsterdam on that little-traveled road. I told him that I did not care and would take my chances and to stop the car right now. When he saw that I meant what I said he first tried to persuade me to stay with him by telling me he would behave himself. I didn't believe him and told him again to stop the car. This time he stopped and let me out. I was happy to be safe and out of his car. I don't think that it took me long to catch a ride and all went well for the remainder of the trip. This was the only time I had problems.

When the Versteegs moved to Amsterdam I had to find another place to live. The new people renting the apartment had enough children and didn't need to rent out any space. The people in the apartment above us told me that they had one room they could rent me, and I could use their toilet. But again, I had to take my showers in the hospital and eat there as well, since I no longer had a kitchen. But it was only for a few months until I got married (more about that later), so I took them up on their offer.

Not long after I moved to my new room, I almost electrocuted myself. I reached behind me to plug something in. The holes in the electrical receptacles in Europe are round and about an eighth inch in diameter. In the Netherlands the voltage is 220; I was feeling around to plug into the wall receptacle and stuck my finger in the wrong hole. Boy, did I get zapped!! I remember how hard it was to pull my finger out of the socket. It blew a fuse and soon the landlord was knocking on my door wondering what I was doing. He wasn't too thrilled because he had to replace the fuse. Needless to say, I was very careful about plugging something in after that experience.

CHAPTER 8

In August 1963, my girlfriend Maaike and I vacationed in Germany. This was the first vacation taken that I could do what I wanted. Even though there were many beautiful things to see in my homeland, its small size and overpopulation stifled me. I wanted to go where there was more room to move around without running into people all the time. I wanted to see trees, flowers, parks and vast, beautiful skies instead of rows and rows of apartment buildings. I wanted to smell fresh air without the fumes of buses and cars and most of all I wanted to go somewhere where everything would be different — the language, the people, the food, and the scenery.

Our first choice was England, but the ferry passage made the trip too expensive. Since we didn't have much money, we decided to visit Germany with its beautiful scenery and its romantic places like the Lorelei and the many castles along the Rhine. Also, both of us were more fluent in German than in English. I think that even then I knew that I didn't want to live in the Netherlands much longer. I wanted to see other parts of the world and hoped by staying on the mainland I would find my Prince Charming who would sweep me off my feet and take me with him for a better life. If I met someone in England, I would be stuck on a big island and feel restricted again.

After we had decided on Germany, I hoped I would find my Prince Charming this first time out of the Netherlands. I took one look in the mirror and realized that he might not find an overweight girl too appealing; I weighed 187 lbs. at that time, which was rather chunky as I am only 5'7" tall. I went on a crash diet and lost 15 pounds in one week by eating only one apple a day and drinking lots of water and coffee. It was a terrible thing to do to my system, but I didn't think it would hurt me as I was young and thought that my body could take a lot of abuse. Losing that weight didn't make me thin by any means, but I did look better. Maaike was one who could eat anything and everything and stay skinny as a rail. How I envied her.

One Sunday morning we left by train from Den Haag and spent a week in Assmanshausen, Germany, a very small, but quaint town on the Rhine. We took a guided tour that lasted from Sunday to Sunday. Most of the people on the trip were already married and were "older" people. By older, I mean anybody older than 30, and most of them were much older than that. We were young and single and didn't want to hang around those "old people" any more than we absolutely had to.

We quickly discovered that the "action" was in Ruedesheim, a small town not too far from Assmanshausen. One picturesque little street named the "Drosselgasse" is famous for its festive atmosphere. Many German songs have been written about Ruedesheim and the Drosselgasse. Not surprisingly, we spent most of our time there. To save money for drinks and souvenirs we relied on hitchhiking to and from our hotel as it was too far to walk. By now I was a pro at traveling that way and we never seemed to have any problem finding a ride. It was during that week that I got drunk for the very first time in my life. I was almost 21 and had never been drunk before. At home, we were never told we couldn't have any alcohol, and in fact we were given watered-down wine on holidays when we were younger regular wine when we were a bit older. I never really cared much for wine and would only take a small sip when a toast was made, just to be sociable. And I never liked beer or hard liquor.

But this was August, and it was very warm — much warmer than living by the coast. We met up with some young guys who invited us to share a glass of wine with them at a sidewalk café. They were paying and we were thirsty, so we had a glass of wine. We were very thirsty, and the wine went down very easily. And soon we had another. We all got along famously so they quickly decided that it would be less expensive if they just bought a couple of bottles in a local grocery store and take them to their campground where we could relax and enjoy ourselves more. We were having fun and agreed to go along with them. It wasn't long before I was so tired, I just fell asleep in their tent. I don't know what Maaike and the young men did, but I was out of it. When I woke up, I didn't feel well. I had my first hangover and didn't get drunk again for another 17 years, which was the second, and so far, the last time in my life. I didn't like how I felt the next day and I don't like to be out of control.

We went on one tour with the "old people," but I don't quite remember where we went that day. While on the tour we met a Russian man who took a liking to me and invited me to go and see the Lorelei with him. The Lorelei is high on top of a mountain and is a statue of a beautiful maiden who, in the past, caused lots of shipwrecks. The people on the boats traveling on the Rhine would look up at her in admiration and couldn't keep their eyes off her. Soon they would crash into the mountain. I did want to see the Lorelei, but not alone with him. He came on too strong and I was afraid of being kidnapped to Russia and never able to leave again. Russia, however beautiful it may be, was not on my list of places to visit or to live. I agreed to meet him, but when he picked me up, I stood at the curb with Maaike and an older couple whom we had befriended. The Russian looked very disappointed, but I insisted that I wouldn't go with him unless they could come along. What could he do? We all got into his car and drove up the steep mountain. I had my first champagne that afternoon. The bubbles made the drink go down easy, but soon I became lightheaded. After we had all enjoyed the view and finished our drinks, we went down the mountain back to our hotel in Assmanshausen where we said our goodbyes. The Russian tried to have some time alone with me, but I graciously declined. I never saw him again.

Later that week on Friday night, Maaike and I visited our favorite place in the Drosselgasse in Ruedesheim, where we had gone almost every night. We were scheduled to return home on Sunday and by Friday night we were nearly broke. We made our drinks last a long, long time, hoping to meet some nice men with lots of money who could make our second to last evening on vacation a fun experience. Our wishes soon came true.

After a while I saw this cute young man sitting across the room from us. He soon came over to our table and introduced himself. His name was Al and obviously was an American. He told us that he was married but that didn't mean he couldn't sit with us. We hit it off from the start. Soon he told us that he had come with a friend and suggested we meet him. I was really looking forward to meeting another American hoping that this one wasn't married and would take a liking to me. I wanted to finish my vacation on a high note even though I would have a much harder time speaking English than if I had met a German man that night. Al introduced his friend. His name was Gary, and they were both in the Air Force, stationed not too far from Ruedesheim. Al sat next to Maaike and soon they were talking and laughing. I wasn't overly impressed with Gary as he was terribly skinny and wore standard military issue glasses which didn't do much for him. Also, he had a crew cut making him look much younger than he was. He looked like a sixteen-year-old and I couldn't imagine what we could do with him, after all we were almost twenty-one years old. Maaike and I decided that we would have to find someone else after we had gotten a couple of drinks from Gary.

Gary sat down next to me and bought me drinks and little souvenirs. Maaike, whose English was much better than mine, chatted with Al as I was smiling and nodding to Gary. My English at that time was not good at all, and understanding American English was even harder. Not much was said between us. We drank some wine, did some dancing and used the universal language of smiling and signing.

As it turned out, Gary and Al had just been paid and had stopped in for a few drinks on their way back from the Air Force library in

Wiesbaden. Gary, being single, had money to buy drinks, while Al couldn't buy too many as he had a wife back in the States. They were hardly the rich Americans we thought they were! Gary was in for a surprise as well. Because my English wasn't very good, I was not very talkative. He thought I was a quiet type of girl who smiled a lot. We danced a few dances but mostly tried to communicate as much as possible. It didn't take him very long, though, to find out that I am not all that quiet.

Before long he told me that he liked me, and not much later he told me that he loved me. How could somebody know that he loves this person he had just met, and who was fat and couldn't even speak the language? Not long before we had to say our good-byes Gary asked me, "Will you marry me?" I didn't really know exactly what he had asked me, but it sounded good. I thought he meant "merry" as in "have a good time." So, I answered "yes." Was I in for a surprise! And a pleasant one, for sure. Gary drove us back to our hotel in his Mercedes which impressed me a lot as I didn't know anybody who had a Mercedes. Gary told me later that it was a very old Mercedes, but it looked good to me. While driving back to the hotel we made a date to meet the next day. That would be our last day in Germany and then we wouldn't see each other for a while.

When Maaike and I got back to our room that night, she was all excited for me. When I asked her why, I was shocked to find out that she had heard Gary propose to me and I had accepted. How could that be? There must have been a mistake somewhere. I had never heard of anyone proposing after such a short time. In the Netherlands it was customary for a couple to date for several months, and then maybe the thought of marriage would be brought up. After I thought about it for a while though, I figured why not take him up on his offer and marry him? It seemed like my ticket to bigger and better things, to get out of the Netherlands, to live where dreams could be realized. Gary had been treating me nicely so far and he didn't seem to care that I was overweight, so I figured this must be the right thing to do.

The next day Gary showed up a couple of hours late. Being late turned out to be a regular habit — one I had to get used to. We had almost given up on seeing him when he and his friend showed up. Gary explained to us that it wasn't his fault because his friend made him late. While on this date he told me again that he wanted to marry me and that he would like to be married as soon as we could. He told me that we could be married in three days if we lived in the States. I could hardly believe my ears. How could that be possible? Anyway, when he got back to the base, we made sure we exchanged addresses and he promised he would write me often. That he did, which was good as I didn't see him for about a month. When he came to visit me the first time, I was a bit worried about walking up to the wrong man. I hardly remembered what he looked like as I didn't have any pictures of him. I didn't need to worry as his haircut and military glasses made him stand out from anyone else. During that visit we set the date to become unofficially engaged on my birthday.

I say "unofficially" as only very few people knew about it. I had told my colleagues in the hospital, but nobody believed me. I had no ring and I had only known him for two days. I hadn't told my parents about him and our plans for marriage, since I hadn't had the nerve to do so. That was to come later. September 18, 1963, was a holiday in the Netherlands that year. Every year, on the third Tuesday in September, the queen rides in her golden carriage for the opening of the new parliament. This is a very festive day with lots of flags hanging everywhere and people watching the golden carriage drive by. That year my birthday fell on the third Tuesday in September. We felt special to have our engagement and my birthday on that day.

Gary kind of panicked at first when I suggested that we become engaged, as he thought that meant he would have to buy a diamond engagement ring. He lucked out because I hadn't seen the beauty and value of a diamond ring yet and told him that a simple gold band would be just fine. He sighed with relief. This was something new to him as a simple golden band is what the groom wears when they get married. In the Netherlands you both wore a golden band on the left hand when you became engaged, and the same band was worn on the right hand when you got married. This was very confusing for Gary. When he went back to the base with a golden band on his left hand everybody thought he was married. Anyway, later I wanted to have a diamond ring but we never had the money for one. The kind I have always wanted was one that you can see without a magnifying glass, so at least a half a carat.

Before we could get married, we needed approval from the U.S. government as well as permission from my parents to marry. Even though I was 21 by then, I needed their consent until I was 30. Without their permission, I could only be married by a judge, and only if he saw no reason to deny our request.

I was afraid my father wouldn't approve. I had brought home a previous boyfriend, Simon, who I thought I really loved. Simon was very tall, well-built and very handsome in his uniform and a very caring person. He was in the Dutch Army and came home on leave every weekend. He and I had been seeing each other for a few months and hit it off very well. However, his parents were not the kind of people my parents approved of because his father was a retired mailman. That did not bother me, but I knew that it bothered my father.

Simon's parents treated me very well and I was often invited over for the evening while Simon was away in his barracks. He had gone straight into the service after high school as was the rule unless one continued with higher education. One day I decided to be brave and take Simon home to meet my parents. It did not take long before my father told him not to come back until he had found a good job and had planned for our future together properly.

Simon had all kinds of plans for the future, but they weren't prestigious enough to suit my family. He planned to be a mechanic — a blue-collar worker considered far below their expectations.

I warned Gary about the visit I had with Simon and the kind of questions my father would ask him. The poor guy was so worried that we decided to stop at a sidewalk cafe and have a couple of beers before the "interview" however, everything turned out all right as Gary wasn't pretentious and didn't make all kinds of promises of things he would or would not do. After a lengthy interview, my father asked Gary to come over for supper the next day and told him that he would give permission to our marriage. I could hardly believe what I heard but was very happy. The only real difference between Gary and Simon was that Gary was in the service and had a good job waiting for him afterward. He was a draftsman, and had a job in Waterloo, Iowa, that paid well considering that he had not completed college.

When Gary came to visit me in the Netherlands, he always had to stay in a nearby hotel. There were no motels in those days yet. He couldn't spend the night with me nor could I spend the night with him. At the hotels, you had to show proof of being married if you planned to spend the night together unless you were older, and people assumed you were married. Without a marriage license, you were simply told that you weren't allowed to even enter your friend's room.

Because I was to marry an American service man, I had to be checked out by the Air Force and the FBI, which included being fingerprinted and filling out mountains of paperwork. Gary visited me in Den Haag every ten days and each time he brought with him more papers to be taken care of. Everything was very official and had to be filled out exactly right. This was not an easy task for a couple who did not speak each other's language fluently enough to know more than just a few simple words. Thank goodness for dictionaries! We probably wore out a couple of them in the first few years.

One time Gary and I had been spending a lot of time filling out paperwork and trying to figure out what needed to be done before the wedding. Before we knew it, it was late, and we ended up falling asleep. We figured that my new landlord wouldn't care since we were engaged and would be married soon. No such luck. No matter how quiet we were that night he found out the next morning what had happened and informed me that I had to leave his home as soon as possible. So,

I moved back home which was not much fun, but where else was I going to find a place to live for three months? Gone was my freedom! Once again, I was back to the rules and regulations of my parents even though I was 21 and engaged to be married. Whenever I left the house, I had to let them know where I was going, who I was going to see and told in no uncertain terms to be home by ten o'clock. It was not easy, but I knew it wouldn't be very long before I would be married and away from them.

Gary wrote to me every day and sometimes even two times a day, so I always had something to look forward to. I didn't realize until later that I wasn't the first one to read Gary's letters. My dad opened every piece of mail that came to the house and read it before giving it to us. He was able to open the letters so well that nobody knew that he had done that. It is a good thing I didn't know that he had been reading my letters until way afterwards. I shouldn't have been surprised, though, because he had read one of my postcards while he was being treated for gall bladder problems in the hospital I was working in. The card had accidentally been given to him instead of being put into my mailbox. Reading a postcard is easy enough to do as one just needs to turn the card over to read it. The card was from my Italian pen-pal and of course my dad didn't approve of that either. I was very upset about that, but since he was quite ill, I didn't make a big deal about it, and afterwards it wasn't worth bringing up. I just had to be extremely careful so it wouldn't happen again. This wasn't easy to do as the mail came to the house while I was at work. I did tell Gary what my dad had done so he was aware of it.

While the police and the FBI were checking me out, Gary (unbeknownst to me) was being investigated as well. Much later I learned later that my father had asked my older brother to find out whatever he could about Gary. My brother was in the Dutch Army, and somehow, he had the means to get the necessary information. Apparently, both of us checked out satisfactorily by all the different people and agencies as we did not have any problems getting married.

In October 1963, I was supposed to take my final exams to become a registered nurse. I passed from the first to the second year, and then from the second to the third year without any problems. However, taking the final exams proved to be a real problem. I just knew that I would never pass even though there was no evidence to support this fear. My fear of failure was revealed every time I had to pass intermediate tests during my nursing program. To pass from one year to the next I had to take a written exam. During the year there were other specific things we were required to learn, and to get them checked off one of the head nurses had to watch how you did that particular procedure. Even though I might have done a procedure many times, and could do it very well, I was always a nervous wreck when the head nurse had to watch me do it. I just knew she would find something wrong with what I did. I always waited as long as possible to perform it in front of her. I did not want to fail. Yet, since I knew I was going to get married anyway, I did the easiest thing I could think of and just quit the program.

Everyone was very surprised and tried to talk me out of quitting, including the head nurse and the superintendent. They told me that I had been such a good nurse and that I would be an asset to the program. Their reaction surprised me even more. I didn't know that they thought so highly of me, as nobody had ever told me that before. I just always tried to do my best and make the patients as comfortable as possible. Wasn't that what you were supposed to do? However, my mind was made up and nobody could change it.

I needed to make some money until I moved to Germany and took a job cleaning house for an American family who lived about five miles away from me. I rode my bike to their house every day and worked from early morning until sometime in the afternoon. This wasn't always too nice as by now it was late fall, early winter and it could be quite cold, windy, and even rainy. Most of the time I arrived at their house shivering from the cold. They had bought two apartments side by side and had taken out the connecting wall. This made it a very big place to live in which was something that impressed me a lot. I didn't know anybody who had that much living space. They had two boys and each boy had his own room. How lucky they were! The boys had turtles for pets and they were allowed to crawl around the apartment. I was happy to have that job as I not only learned the American language a little better but also learned some American family customs. It was a bit hard understanding what the wife wanted me to do, especially in the beginning. But she pointed at what needed to be done and somehow, I figured it out.

At any rate, I thought the American family was very nice and treated me well. However, my father, as usual, found something to criticize right away. As soon as I arrived for work, I was supposed to set the table for the family's breakfast and get everything ready. Once they sat down to eat, I had to go back into the kitchen where I could eat my breakfast. This is what my father objected to. He thought I should have been able to sit down with them and be treated as an equal. At lunchtime I ate with the lady of the house, and we chatted about a variety of things; that is to say, she did most of the talking and I tried to understand what she was saying. She was thin and tried to show me how I could lose weight, if I wanted to, by eating the way she was eating.

One time, shortly after I started working for her, she came home from the store and asked me if I had made the beds. This totally confused me as I did not see anything wrong with how I made the bed, and certainly would not have known how to fix it. I soon learned what she really meant by her question. I thought she meant repair the beds. There was so much to be learned about the American language, things that can be very confusing to a foreigner.

Fortunately, I had no problems with how I was treated, as the family was very nice to me. One time I cut my thumb really bad while drying off a glass and she told me to go to the hospital to get it taken care of. She wrapped a cloth around it and off I went. When I arrived in the hospital, I was taken care of immediately. It helps if everybody knows you. They poured some kind of liquid in a shallow dish and told me to put my thumb in it. The problem was that the only way my wound would touch the liquid was if I bent my thumb in such a way that it was at a 90-degree angle towards my wrist. They were very surprised that I could do that, and I soon found out that not everybody could do that. I was surprised about that because I couldn't figure out how other people could get the liquid to touch their wound if they had a similar cut.

On November 23, I heard the shocking news that President Kennedy had been assassinated. I became very worried. I never realized that regular people could carry guns or other weapons of destruction, and now the President was dead. How could that happen to somebody that powerful? If he couldn't be protected, what would it be like for everyday citizens? Was life really about like the movies I had seen where people just shoot others? What was I getting myself into? How many people walked around with guns in their pockets or purses? Would I have to learn to defend myself as well? Was I making the right decision to leave the Netherlands? It was small and cramped but there wasn't any crime to speak of. It made a big impression on me. Gary would have to answer many questions next time he came. Gary explained as much as he could and told me that I needn't worry. This had been a political thing and wasn't an everyday occurrence. It made me feel a little more relieved and the wedding was still on.

Gary came from Germany for Christmas and brought a big turkey with him. My mother had never cooked a turkey before. They probably had eaten turkey before but in Indonesia the cooks had prepared them and in the Netherlands they couldn't afford to eat fowl. Gary helped her prepare and bake the turkey and everyone enjoyed the meal. We felt very rich having such a wonderful meal. Since people in America give presents for Christmas, I had knitted a nice scarf for Gary. He was very impressed that I could do something like that and has always treasured it.

If I remember correctly, he couldn't stay for New Year's Eve, which was a pity as this is always an exciting time in the Netherlands. Everybody buys fireworks and shoots them off at midnight. Any kind of firework is legal in the Netherlands. It was a lot of fun, but also dangerous. Every year accidents would happen and sometimes they were very severe. Many people, including children, would lose an eye or a finger. But that wouldn't stop the people from shooting them off though. I liked the ones that made a lot of noise or that were very colorful. Of course, you would have to try out some of the fireworks beforehand, so you knew which ones to buy a quantity of before New Year's Eve. Most people would start shooting them off several days ahead, and then would buy more of the ones they liked to be sure they had plenty of them on hand for New Year's Eve.

Sometimes kids would throw firecrackers in people's mailboxes. Some mailboxes are just slots that the mailman would slip the mail through into the homes. If you lived in an area where kids would do that, you made sure that your mailbox slots were secure and would not open.

At midnight you would hear a lot of fireworks around you as people were gathered around with their glass of wine, champagne or beer to wish everybody a happy and healthy New Year. I sure missed all of that; it just didn't seem the same without fireworks to welcome the New Year.

Soon it was February and getting closer and closer to our wedding day. My mother was busy making me a two-piece suit out of dark blue material with a black pattern in it. She had told me that I couldn't have a white dress because I was too fat. I again weighed 187 pounds, so I was by no means skinny, but I didn't think I was too fat to have a beautiful white dress with a train and veil. For a long time before and after the wedding I looked in wedding magazines and dreamed about what it would feel like to wear one of those beautiful dresses. I didn't dare touch a real dress as it would have made me cry.

I think the real reason my mother insisted that I wear a suit was that a true bridal gown would have been much more expensive than the two-piece suit she made for me. There was a possibility that my dream would come true even though the chance of that happening was slim. Maaike's brother was getting married in December, two months before us, and his future wife told me that I could borrow her dress if

I could fit into it. It was a nice offer, to be sure, but she weighed sixty pounds less than I did and there was no safe way I could lose that much weight in a short time. So, the blue suit was the only option. Besides that, I could never lose weight when there is a lot of stress in my life, and I had plenty to contend with. We also had to find an appropriate hat and shoes to wear on my wedding day. I sure wasn't going to look like a beautiful bride but that is how it was going to be.

Even though I didn't get to have the dress I really wanted, it was still a very exciting time for me. I remember how much I looked forward to February 18th, hoping that the weather would be nice. February tends to be very cold and dreary and often it would rain. If I couldn't have the dress and the shoes that I dreamed of, then I would just hope for a sunny and cheery day, and that everything would go smoothly. But it also was very nerve-wracking. After all, my whole life would be so different. Would I be able to adjust to this new life in this new country far away from everything and everyone I knew?

CHAPTER 9

On February 18, 1964, we were married by a Justice of the Peace in Den Haag, my hometown. It was hardly the wedding I had dreamed of. We did not get married in a church because neither of us belonged to one. To make any marriage legal in the Netherlands a civil marriage ceremony is always required. A church ceremony by itself does not make it a legal marriage.

It didn't take me very long to get dressed in my "wedding suit." Even though my mother had done a very nice job and the suit fit me very well, I didn't feel like I was getting married. After all, the bride wears a white wedding gown, and the rest of the guests wear suits or dresses. I felt awkward in my suit with my hat and purse that were especially bought for this special day. Since I didn't have a veil nor wore make-up there wasn't anything special about getting dressed.

Ours was a very small wedding because my parents didn't have much money, nor did we. Only very close friends and family were invited. I felt bad not being able to invite all my friends and having them there with me on this special day. It would have been so nice to have them there with me especially since I would soon be moving to Germany for the remainder of Gary's tour of duty and then to the United States. There wasn't much time to spend with them; everything seemed so rushed. Also, we got married on a Monday, a workday, and it was harder for people to take off from work. Getting married on

Monday was cheaper than getting married on Friday or Saturday – hence the Monday wedding.

We were to be married in the morning, and as usual Gary was late showing up. In fact, he was so late that my poor father was beginning to wonder if there was going to be a wedding. To this day Gary claims it wasn't his fault that he was late. His two friends, Jimmy and George, who were to be the best man and witness decided at the last moment to get haircuts. Why couldn't they have done that the day before or before they left the base, I wondered? Gary would have called us to let us know that he was to be late, but we didn't have a telephone and he didn't know the number of the neighbor downstairs. Finally, everybody arrived, and we all went to the courthouse.

In the Netherlands the whole ceremony is totally different than here. The groom picks up the bride and they go together to the church or courthouse to get married. So, the groom gets to see what the bride looks like in her gown or dress before they get to the church or courthouse. Normally the couple would have been in a taxi, or a horse drawn carriage, but since we didn't have the means for that we had to do it the cheap way. This meant that Gary drove us in his 1961 Renault Gordini, a small car, to the city hall. His friends George and Jimmy sat in the backseat. My dad had rented a couple of taxis for him and our family; however, there was no room for George and Jimmy. My wish about the weather came through though, as the sun was shining and it was not too cold.

If my memory serves me right, the ceremony was very short and didn't take more than fifteen minutes. The wedding party waits in the hall until it is their turn to get married. When the couple is married there are a couple of minutes to congratulate the bride and groom, and then everybody leaves the room on the opposite side from where they came in. In the meantime, the next couple is waiting to enter the room to get married — assembly line style.

The ceremony was first in Dutch and then in English; this was to accommodate Gary who didn't understand much Dutch yet. I was completely caught up in the whole proceedings listening to every word that was said. But then the English version started and since I didn't understand much English I soon got lost and started not paying attention too much. I finally became aware of what was going on again because my family kept telling me to say, "I do."

I suppose they were all wondering if I was having second thoughts. Of course, I said "yes," and so I was now Mrs. Maricle. After the wedding, we all went to a small, but nice restaurant and had lunch. During the lunch, my father made a little speech, and that's when I saw him shed a few tears. I was surprised and confused by this display of emotion, as I really didn't think that he loved me that much and I never really had seen tears in his eyes. I learned later that he did love me very much, but just couldn't or wouldn't show it. And his tears were there because he knew he wouldn't see me much after I got married.

We were able to go on a honeymoon thanks to the American people I worked for. Even though I had only worked for them for a mere few months and wouldn't work there much longer after I was married, they gave me a whole week off with pay so Gary and I could start our life together as husband and wife. We thought that was very kind indeed. They told me to keep in touch after I moved to Germany, and I am sorry to say that I did not do that.

Soon we were on our way to Berchtesgaden, Germany, for our honeymoon. Gary's friends had to ride with us back to Hahn Air Force Base as they didn't have any other way to get back. Hardly the kind of wedding they have in the States where they throw rice when you leave the church, put cans behind your car, and you drive off by yourselves to start your new life. But we were married! We planned to drop them off at the base on our way to Berchtesgaden, but things didn't start out well at all. It is a good thing we weren't superstitious.

We hadn't even left Den Haag yet when the muffler fell off our car. It was a long, noisy six-hour drive to the base. Not only did we have two people sitting in the back of us, but the noise of the muffler was too loud to carry on any conversation. We were lucky that we didn't get stopped by the Dutch police, or the German border patrol, as we would have gotten a ticket. After we dropped off Gary's friends at the base, we went to a little town nearby to spend the night. On the way over, we had a flat tire. The next day we had to find a mechanic who could fix the muffler and the tire before we could continue our trip. We were finally on our way again when in Munich one of the spark plugs came out. Gary was able to put it back somehow so we could be on our way again. I soon learned how handy he was — he seemed to be able to fix anything and at any time. By the time we arrived in Berchtesgaden, it was very late at night.

Berchtesgaden is high up in the mountains and there was a lot of fog that evening. We kept driving around in circles trying to find our hotel, always ending up at the same spot. Since Gary didn't want to ask for directions I finally decided to do so. Gary didn't speak much German and I was fluent enough in it to ask for directions and to be able to understand what they said. Exhausted, but happy, we finally found our hotel. I don't remember doing much sightseeing, but I know we did go to the salt mines in Salzburg as I still have the little box with samples of salt in them. And we took the ski lift to get a better view of the area but there was so much fog you could hardly see anything.

One of the most memorable incidents occurred in the bathtub. We were taking a bath together, enjoying the luxury of a nice hot bath, and some well-deserved time by ourselves. The next thing we knew, the maid was standing in the bathroom. She had knocked on the door of the room to see if she could make the bed and nobody had answered. So, she let herself in and caught us by surprise. She should have heard us, as we weren't being that quiet, but her arrival certainly ended our relaxation time in the tub. We also had to send everybody a postcard from Berchtesgaden as this was the proper thing to do whenever you go on vacation and even on your honeymoon. I remember sitting on the terrace on one of the few sunny days and writing them.

On Sunday we drove back to Den Haag and Gary left for the base. I was to follow him a week or so later after he had found an apartment for us and had made all the arrangements to begin our lives together. I could hardly wait to be with him and was wondering why he hadn't done so before. In the meantime, I went back to work for the American family.

Soon he returned to take me back to Germany. I was finally leaving the Netherlands and would be starting a new life. One of the first things we had to do was to go on base and make arrangements for having his check divided in half so one half was made out to me and the other half to him. I was curious what the reason for that was, and Gary explained to me that they had to do this because some service men would spend too much money on themselves and not leave enough money for the wife to buy groceries and things she might need. That was nice but if the husband was that way wouldn't he just make her give the money to him after she cashed the check? The whole thing seemed silly to me. And I felt kind of weird taking a check for something I hadn't worked for. But that was the way it was.

The Air Force had another rule I couldn't quite understand. In order for me to get into one of their stores I had to wear a skirt; I wasn't allowed to wear slacks. I found this out the hard way the first time we drove to a base near Wiesbaden. I remember it was a very cold day and I had worn slacks to keep warm. When we were trying to get into the store we were stopped and told that I couldn't enter since I had slacks on. Gary explained the situation and we were allowed in just this once.

One thing that was very hard to get used to was the fact that everybody called each other by their first names right away. Even children called me by my first name instead of Mrs. Maricle. And, once I started working, I even had to call my supervisors by their first name. That was totally unheard of where I came from. Children would never call an adult by their first name and adults would need to give another adult permission to have them call them by their first name. That is all different now in the Netherlands and the same as in America, but I had a hard time with it then.

Another thing I noticed right away about the American people was that everybody seemed to drive a car and a lot of the people driving cars seemed so very young. They couldn't be more than fifteen or so. I soon found out that one could get a driver's license at age sixteen. I was in awe as I had tried to learn to drive a car before I got married but had to give it up after three lessons. During my first lesson I was taught how to start the car, put it in first gear, and drive away slowly. The second lesson taught me shifting into second and third gear. By the third lesson, I was driving in actual downtown traffic. I still remember the morning I tried to find my way through the noon rush hour amongst the streetcars, buses, bicycles, and other automobiles. At one point I had to stop for a red light and the instructor told me to step on the brake. I was so nervous that I completely forgot which pedal was the brake and which one was the gas. I nearly gave my poor instructor a heart attack when I pushed with all my might on the gas pedal. Fortunately for all of us, he was able to stay in control and stepped on the brake and we stopped just in time. We didn't stay in that part of town much longer. I decided that driving a car was too hard for me to learn so I quit taking lessons. I was good at rationalizing and told myself that I didn't need to learn to drive because of the excellent transportation system and that I would never be able to afford my own car anyway.

So, when I saw all these American teenagers driving these big cars, I figured they must all be super smart, definitely much smarter than I was. However, one thing we could do in the Netherlands that they couldn't, was drinking alcohol at age sixteen. They couldn't drink until they were twenty-one at that time. It was very hard for me to understand why someone could drive a car, get married at age eighteen and fight for his country but couldn't have a drink once in a while. They could drink alcohol on base, but never off base. This didn't make sense either.

Everybody seemed to be very rich because each family had a car, and I thought that you had to be rich to have a car. There was so much I still needed to learn.

A trip to the grocery store was quite an eye opener. First, the grocery stores themselves were huge compared to the little stores I shopped in before I moved to Germany. Then I couldn't believe the size of the packages the food came in. Everything seemed so large, especially the trays of meat and the size of the cereal boxes. And there were so many cereals from which to choose. How could you possibly select from all those choices? And everything seemed to be in such abundance. I could certainly get used to that! If that was how life was going to be living in the U.S.A., I was happy. I soon found out though that people don't buy groceries every day like we did in the Netherlands.

Our first apartment in Germany was in a tiny town named Loetzbeuren. I think it only had about 100 inhabitants, one grocery story and two taverns. Since I came from a town of at least 400,000, this was a big change for me. This was as rural an area as I had ever seen, and I felt very isolated from civilization.

We shared a house with another young couple who both worked on base, too. She was French, and even though they weren't married yet, they were living together. This was very unusual in those days; at least the way I was brought up. They soon had to get married, however, because their first baby was due in October. They invited us to their wedding which took place in or around Paris but, unfortunately, we were not able to go. We had to save every penny as we had to buy my plane ticket to the United States. We did go to the movies on base two or three times a week as it was very inexpensive (only $0.25 per person), and this way I would learn more about American life and a few words here and there.

We had the upstairs apartment and the other couple lived downstairs. They shared the bath with us but had their own toilet. In order for anyone to take a bath someone had to build a fire in the water heater and keep it going for at least one hour. This was very inconvenient as we had to give up some of our privacy during the time they heated the water and then took their baths.

Cooking in our kitchen was done the same way — by building a fire in the wood burning stove. Since neither one of us had ever cooked that way before, it was an impossible task at first. Even I hadn't learned that way of cooking in the "huishoud school." During the summer, we did not want to heat up the whole kitchen to cook a meal or even make some coffee.

There was another way of cooking which was equally hard for me as well. We had a two-burner electric stove which was totally foreign to me as we only had gas stoves in the Netherlands. The burners were about one-inch thick and solid (no rings in it) and they took forever to heat up. And once the burner was hot, it seemed to take forever to cool down; and it certainly was very hard to control. I hadn't done much cooking before, and when I did it had been on a gas stove. I did my share of burning the meals during the short time I cooked. To this day I still prefer cooking on gas because of the control you have with it, even though the newer electric stoves heat up almost as fast as gas.

To wash the dishes, we had to heat up the water either on the wood stove or on the electric stove and rinsing was done with cold water. Rinsing the dishes was a new experience for me and seemed rather wasteful. We never rinsed the dishes in the Netherlands; one would just wipe them dry. But Gary insisted that I do it, saying that it wasn't a healthy practice to wipe the suds into the dishes.

The apartment itself was rather roomy. The living room had a little kerosene stove in it, the bedroom was plenty large, and the kitchen was big enough to have a big dining room table in it. If it wasn't for the inconvenience of sharing the bath, the wood kitchen stove, and firing up the water heater before taking a bath, it would have been great.

It didn't take long before I found out I was pregnant. We were both very excited about it and were wondering what the baby would look like. At the same time, we were also nervous about becoming parents, as we didn't have any close family nearby to help us with any questions we might have. I think the added anxiety caused me to have morning sickness, as in my case I was sick 24 hours a day. The thought or smell of food made me sick and even looking at a picture of food made me very nauseous. I lost 30 pounds the first month of my pregnancy. I couldn't eat or drink anything other than very small amounts of water for the first month and then very little afterwards. Poor Gary tried very hard to find something that I could eat and that wouldn't make me vomit, but he had no luck. We had an Oriental Air Force doctor, and he wasn't a bit worried about my weight loss. He said that I was big enough, and the baby would take from me whatever it needed. Wouldn't that deplete me, I wondered? He didn't seem to think so. However, he did give me some pills to take for the morning sickness, but I threw them up almost as fast as they were swallowed. This was probably good as I don't believe in taking medications and especially not when pregnant.

The next two months were somewhat better, but I still could not eat much and then only limited types of food. I never really regained my appetite during my pregnancy and didn't have any cravings for pickles or other strange things other women were craving. My big thing was Baby Ruth candy bars although my favorite candy bar used to be a Mars bar. I had never eaten Baby Ruth candy bars before I became pregnant and haven't eaten them since. I just don't seem to like them enough to eat them.

Then there was Oma who made life very interesting, to say the least. Oma was the mother of the landlady who lived in the house next door; in fact, the entire family lived in that house. Their house and ours were connected on opposite sides of the barn. Oma kept a key to our apartments and came in whenever she wanted, even when we weren't home. In Germany the landlord could come in at any time without permission to check up on things. The apartment was furnished and was quite comfortable. We did not like the way the furniture was arranged in the living room, however, so we arranged things the way we liked and never gave it a second thought. One day we came home after being gone all day, and to our big surprise we found our furniture rearranged back the way it was before we moved in. I soon knew exactly what it feels like when somebody breaks into your apartment. Except in our case nothing was missing, but we still felt that our privacy had been invaded. We quickly rearranged it back the way we wanted it and enjoyed the arrangement until the next time we were gone for the day. The same thing happened again. We tried to explain to Oma that we wanted things our way and that we really didn't appreciate her coming into our apartment when we weren't there, but she did not care.

Oma also insisted that we wash all the windows inside and out every week. We didn't though. There was no way I was going to climb the ladder or hang out the windows that often. Besides that, the next time it rained they would get dirty again and it rained often enough for me not to wash the windows every week. Gary did all the cleaning of the apartment as I was in no shape to do any of that. We had wood floors that needed to be waxed regularly. This was quite a chore as one had to put the wax on first and then take this real heavy wax block and push it back and forth across the floor. That thing was so heavy I could hardly move it, but it did a good job making the floor nice and shiny.

I was often home alone at night because Gary worked rotating shifts. Oma would sometimes come over uninvited to have coffee or hot chocolate with me. One time she came and almost scared me to death. I had not heard her come up the stairs and suddenly, I heard a knock on my door. The door was right on the top of the stairs and when I opened it, I did not see anyone. The staircase was dark, and she hadn't turned the light on and neither had I. I was about ready to shut the door thinking I must have heard wrong when she started talking to me. I still did not see her, so I looked around and found her sitting on the steps several stairs down. She wanted to know when we were going back to the Netherlands again because she needed more coffee. She liked the Dutch coffee better than the German coffee and always ordered some to bring back to her.

Then there were the cows and the spiders and the mice. In the early evening the farmers brought their cows into the barn to spend the night only to take them to the fields again the next morning. They thought that the cows couldn't be outside all night as they might get cold and wet and would get sick. At night we could hear the cows scraping their hoofs and horns against the walls — something to get used to for this city girl. Day and night we heard mice running in between the walls. I was terribly afraid of mice but as soon as I was assured that they stayed behind the walls I quit worrying about them. Initially I didn't believe that these mice would stay within the walls, but I must say, I never saw any in our apartment.

My greater concern became the spiders. These spiders were huge and when they got squashed blood would splatter all over the place. Even though they weren't poisonous, at least we didn't think so, I didn't like them at all. One evening Gary had just left for work and wouldn't be home until early morning hours. I saw a big spider on the wall behind my bed and was petrified and didn't know what to do. Then I quickly looked outside the window to see if I could catch Gary and have him kill it, but he was already gone. If I tried to hit him and missed, he might crawl away, and I might not find him until he was in our bed. So, that wasn't an alternative. The only other alternative was to sit there and watch him, hoping the thing would crawl away into the wall or through a crack and to the outside. Of course, if that happened the spider could crawl back out again, but I didn't want to think about that. I had no luck as he just sat there, and I watched him sit there. I don't think I slept much that night and was very happy to see Gary when he came home after work.

All this was still not as bad as the big manure pile right under our bedroom window. It came about halfway up the wall right smack underneath the window and after a big rain its aroma would rise up into our apartment and stay there for a long time. It was enough to make a person sick. I wonder if I would have had fewer problems with being sick during the first three months of my pregnancy if I hadn't had to smell those vapors all day long.

Another bad thing about the apartment was that the kitchen, where we ate our meals, faced the back yard. This would have been a wonderful thing to look at while eating our meals. But in the back yard was the outhouse used by the farmer and the family next door. It was not so bad when the women used it as they always closed the door behind them. The men, however, didn't bother and provided us with a very unappetizing view while we were eating our meals. They just didn't seem to care. We soon learned to just look the other way while they were doing their job.

Doing the laundry was another big chore. We had to save every penny we could and therefore had to wash the clothing, bedding, etc., by hand in the bathtub. Of course, this meant that we had to build a fire in the water heater first. I sure couldn't help much, being sick all the time and losing all that weight. Soon it became too much for Gary as well, so wound up going to the Laundromat on base, and then brought the wash back home to be hung up either outside or, on rainy days, in the attic. We couldn't afford to let the dryer dry our clothes, so we had to hang them in the attic to dry. The attic was something else as well. It was dark and musty and had all kinds of creepy stuff sitting around. I never was too excited to be there to hang up the wash or take it down. But the money we didn't use for a dryer, we could use for other things.

While we lived in Loetzbeuren Maaike came to visit us and stayed for a few days. It was so nice to have her there especially while Gary was at work. We had been best friends, and this gave us a chance to catch up with what had been going on in our lives. She also visited us once in the 60s while we were living in Arizona. Unfortunately, we have lost contact.

We did not stay very long in Loetzbeuren and in the fall we moved to Sohren, a somewhat bigger town. There we rented the upstairs as well and our downstairs neighbors were our landlady and her family. Since this was a little bigger town, there were no barns or cows in it. Things were better in many ways. We had a little electric water heater over the kitchen sink. I think it held only a gallon, but with the push of a button we would have hot water very fast. At least we could wash dishes more easily and make coffee or tea faster. We still shared the bathroom, but this time it was downstairs, and nobody had to come into our apartment. This family respected our privacy, too, and did not come upstairs unless they had been invited. Also, this landlady insisted that I didn't wash the windows or stretch up high to hang curtains or reach for high things. She said that it was too dangerous in my condition and offered to do it for me. Very few people believed that I was going to have a baby soon as I was much thinner than they expected me to be.

The only bad thing about this apartment was that the landlord and landlady raised their grandson there. His parents both worked and lived a couple of hours away and chose not to be involved with their son any more than they had to. The boy was too small to go to school or pre-school yet and stayed with his grandparents all day. I don't remember him going very often to play with other children. or that other children came over to play with him. I wondered how he could have the kind of experiences other kids did. His parents did not come over to see him very often. In Europe a two-hour trip to visit someone is a big deal and not done too often. The boy must have been bored silly as he cried and fussed a lot and had a terrible temper. I would have played with him except I didn't think I could speak enough German to be understood. Besides that, I didn't have all that much energy to play with such a young child. I still couldn't eat much and had never regained the weight I had lost during the first months of my pregnancy.

While we were living in Sohren, my younger brother and sister spent a week or so with us. They had come by train, and I planned to go back by train with them to visit my family and friends. It was nice to have them with us as now, and I had someone to talk to in my own language. I didn't have to strain and think what and how I was going to communicate. I also had companionship while Gary was at work. I seemed to be alone a lot and really didn't have enough to do to keep me occupied. Yet, I couldn't do any of the things an expectant mother would normally do such as making the baby's room ready, buying the clothes, the crib, the playpen, the stroller etc. Our baby would be born not long before I had to immigrate to America, and I certainly couldn't take all those things with me. So, we walked a lot in the neighborhood and to the base, which was a couple of miles from our apartment. We sometimes rode back with Gary when he got off work, or we would walk home if we didn't want to wait for him and we felt up to it. My new landlady didn't like that too much as she thought I was overdoing it by walking so far. But by then I felt well enough to do all the walking, and I figured it would be good for me.

All three of us were afraid of spiders, and even though we didn't have a manure pile under our window we still had plenty of spiders occupying our apartment. One afternoon when Gary was at work, we discovered a big spider on the living room wall. My brother and sister had never seen a spider that size before. I told them about what a terrible mess you made if you squashed a spider like that. The blood would splatter all over the wall and would be hard to clean up afterwards. None of us dared to kill the thing by smashing it for fear that we would miss and the terrible mess it would make if we did hit it. Neither one of us wanted to try to catch it and throw it outside — it was just too big and scary. We had a can of bug spray and figured that a couple of sprays would kill the critter. We didn't really want to do that as the spray would not be too good for me to inhale given my condition. But what else could we do? The only problem was that bug spray didn't affect this spider, and it just kept crawling around. We sprayed and sprayed and sprayed, but nothing happened. Finally, Gary came home and could not believe his eyes. The room was full of bug spray, and there were three adults waiting for him to kill the spider, as they were too afraid to do so. To this day he talks about that. Anyway, he killed the spider and quickly opened the windows to get rid of the fumes.

Finally, the day came that all three of us were to go back to the Netherlands. I hadn't been home for a while and was looking forward to seeing the city and my friends and family again. Our parents knew which train we would be on and when to expect us home. We took the bus to Koblenz where we would catch the train to Den Haag. I never was good at riding in a bus or car and always became quite sick. While I was pregnant the problem was even worse. We sat down behind some kids that took that same bus to go to school — I guess they didn't have school buses. They were all dressed up nicely and were talking and laughing. All of a sudden, I became very sick to my stomach and had to throw up. It all happened so fast that I couldn't move to a safe place to vomit. I ended up throwing up all over the boy in front of me. My sister and brother were so embarrassed, and I wasn't very happy either, but I really could not have prevented it. The boy never turned around to show his displeasure, nor did he or his friends next to him say anything to us. I'm sure they were quite upset about the whole situation but got off at their regular stop to walk the rest of the way to school. I wonder if that poor boy had to wear those stinky clothes all day or if he somehow got cleaned up. I really felt bad about what happened but didn't know what I could have done at the time.

For some reason we missed the train and took the next one. We didn't know how to call our parents from the train station in Koblenz as we were very illiterate about telephones, and they didn't have a telephone. They never had had a telephone in their apartment until after I lived in America. I only knew one girl whose parents had a telephone and that was not until I was almost eighteen years old. Before that none of our friends or family had a telephone. We would have had to call a neighbor who had one and we didn't know who that might be. Not thinking that it was really that important to let anybody know that we had taken a later train, we just waited for the next one and enjoyed our trip home.

We didn't know how lucky we were to be on the later train. And we didn't realize the agony we put our parents through by not letting them know about our change of travel plans. We learned later that the train that we should have taken had crashed with another train and there had been quite a few casualties. My parents knew about it as it had been on the news, but we did not know anything about it at all. I still remember how surprised and happy my parents looked when the three of us walked in the door. They had thought that all of us were dead and their first grandchild to be born to them was dead, too.

Mr. Versteeg, his wife and their three children came to visit us in Germany as well. They had a pop-up van and slept in it while with us since we did not have room for them and their children. Somehow it all worked out great and it was nice to have people come to see us. We had made some friends on base, but having family and friends from home was just a little more special. We had a great time with them and showed them around the area as much as we could. And my friend Maaike came again and spent some time with us. It was so nice to see her again and to reminisce about old times. It seems we never got caught up talking about our lives.

On the morning of January 14, 1965, I felt something pop inside me and suddenly a big gush of liquid was released. I really didn't know what was going on, but I knew I should go to the hospital. I wasn't at all prepared for delivering a baby. During my nurse's training I had not worked in the maternity ward, so I still didn't really know what to expect. Gary, of course, wasn't any more knowledgeable than I so he wasn't much help either. I sure wish some kind soul had been there with me to help me through it all. We quickly drove to the base hospital. In those days husbands weren't allowed in the delivery room, but he could come in the room I was in before I delivered. However, Gary doesn't handle hospital situations well at all and wasn't much help. My mother, sister, or any of my friends lived too far away to come to my aid. The nurses in the air force hospital weren't very kind at all. When I cried because I was in pain, they told me to be quiet and that a first delivery usually lasted about 18 hours. I sure wasn't prepared for that, nor did I think I could last that long with the amount of pain I was experiencing. Our little girl, Marian, was born after about eight hours which seemed like an eternity for me. But when I saw her, like any other new mom, I soon forgot about the pain. Marian was a beautiful baby with no wrinkles, and she had lots of long, red hair, and big blue eyes. I was totally confused about the red hair as neither Gary nor I had red hair, but Gary explained quickly that his mother had red hair. She weighed seven pounds, ten ounces, which was more than I would have expected her to be. I had lost 30 pounds the first month of my pregnancy and never gained any of it back the rest of the time I was pregnant. I lost another 20 pounds delivering her, which brought me to my ideal weight immediately after giving birth. In fact, I was so thin after the delivery that the people in Germany didn't think I had ever been pregnant or had delivered a baby. My tummy was flat immediately.

After Marian's birth I had exactly one month to get ready for my move to the States. Gary was getting discharged shortly before that. We had to get Marian's birth certificate and passport. Our little girl had a passport when she wasn't even one month old. How cool is that? I had to pack the few belongings we could take with us and sell or give away the rest. We were severely limited in what luggage we could take as we didn't have the money to send everything we wanted to keep back to the States, even if we would send it by boat. Trying to decide what to take and what to leave behind was extremely hard for me. These were things given to me less than a year ago and were from dear friends and family members. Now I had to leave them behind. I must have had similar feelings of what my parents had gone through when they went to the camps and were told they could only take with them what they could carry. Maybe it was a lesson for me to leave old baggage behind and to start out fresh in a new country.

Because Gary was an enlisted man in the service less than four years and not an officer or non-commissioned officer, we had to pay for my airfare. Fortunately, Marian could fly for free as she was an infant under two years old. We had lived very frugally to save up for the flight. I remember we often bought a big head of cabbage which lasted a whole week. Once a week we treated ourselves to a small flank steak. That became a tradition we kept for a long time and still buy occasionally for old memories. During our stay in Germany my cousin invited us to visit her in Norway where she and her husband were living at that time. Unfortunately, we couldn't afford to spend the money on gasoline, hotel, and ferry to get there — something we later regretted.

However, the money had to be saved or spent on real necessities. We knew that and learned to live with it.

On February 1, 1965, Gary and a friend drove us back to the Netherlands. Marian and I would stay there for a couple of weeks with my parents before our actual trip to the United States. Gary would fly back on February 9, to get his discharge from the Air Force. My family and friends were able to see me and Marian for just a short time, only a couple of weeks. My parents were so happy to see me and meet their very first grandchild. A few days before we left for the USA, I had Marian checked over by the pediatrician my mother knew; just to make sure everything was fine before undertaking the long trip abroad. She was eating well and was a very happy baby. She hardly ever cried and was perfectly content with her new surroundings. She checked out okay. On February 14, the day before I immigrated, I received a big Valentine's Day card from Gary saying he missed us, and he looked forward to seeing us soon. We didn't do much of anything for Valentine's Day at that time as money was still mostly spent on necessities. I was very surprised to get such a big card.

And then, finally, the big day came — February 15, 1965 — the day I immigrated to the United States! The day which I had waited for so long!

CHAPTER 10

I don't remember much of all that happened on February 15, 1965. It seems so long ago, and it was such a chaotic time. I know that we had to get up early to be at the airport on time. The night before our departure my mother had taken Marian in her room with her so I could get more sleep; this was a very nice gesture, but I don't think I slept much that night anyway. All I could think about was my last year and all the things that had happened in such a short time. I got married, moved to Germany where they spoke a different language, we lived in two different apartments, I became pregnant and had a baby, learned to speak some English, got to know some of the customs of Americans and Germans, and I had to prepare for immigration to America. And now I was moving to America. I probably maxed out on the stress scale. All this was going through my head making it very hard to get a decent night sleep. Needless to say, I was very tired when I had to get up.

The tiredness soon went away when the realization of what was about to happen set in. I had never been in an airport or even close to an airplane. Everything was new to me and many new, wonderful experiences were ahead of me as well. There were also plenty of sad feelings because of leaving behind everyone and everything that I had known so far. It was almost too much to handle, but I had to be strong for my family and friends, and for my little girl.

Schiphol, the airport near Amsterdam, was a good hour's drive from our house. We didn't own a car nor did we know anybody who did, so we had to rely on a taxi, bus, or train. Going by bus turned out to be the cheapest. My whole family came to the airport with us to make sure that everything went smoothly and to be with us as long as possible. We first took a local bus that dropped us off at the KLM shuttle bus stop in downtown Den Haag which took us to the airport. Once we arrived at Schiphol Mr. Versteeg and his whole family was there to meet us, as promised.

Even though there were lots of different emotions going on inside me, I also felt excited knowing that we were going to America. This is something I had always dreamed of, and hoped for, but never thought would happen. At the same time, I didn't know if and when I would see my family or friends again. Even though I was never close to my family, it still was a sobering thought to leave them that far behind. After all, they weren't young anymore, especially my father who was almost 68. And in the sixties, one didn't travel overseas very often. It was too expensive and too big an undertaking.

We finally said our goodbyes at the gate. This was the second time that I saw my dad shed a few tears; I'm not sure if anyone else cried, but I'm sure they were all very sad. Even though I was very sad to leave everyone behind, I couldn't cry. I was too excited about what was ahead of me and had to control myself to make sure I got on the right airplane. Thinking back, I was struggling with old commands from the camp years: "don't cry, don't show your emotions." which is something I still have a hard time doing.

I still remember walking up the stairs into the plane in awe. I kept wondering how something that big could possibly leave the ground and then stay up in the air all the way across the ocean. Why wouldn't it fall like anything else that is thrown up high in the sky? Maybe I should have paid more attention in my science class? At the same time, I had this naive trust that everybody knew what they were doing and nothing could possibly go wrong. The stewardess was very helpful and led me to my seat. Since I flew KLM, the crew all spoke Dutch. Marian was put in her little travel basket, which had served as her bed, and was hung above my head. The next thing I heard were the instructions on how to exit the plane and what to do if we were going to have to land on the water. I then started to realize the certainty of everything and became more nervous. I asked myself: "You mean there is actually a chance that this plane could fall from the sky?" What a horrible thought, and how could we survive if we would fall into the ocean? What would happen to Marian? How could I save her?

Marian must have picked up my shift of emotions as she cried the whole eight hours until we landed in New York City. Normally she hardly ever cried. The more she cried the more nervous and embarrassed I became, and the more nervous and embarrassed I became, the more she cried. People were looking at me wondering why I couldn't do something to quiet her down. Finally, we started to descend, and I got ready to leave the plane by trying to put on my shoes. I didn't know that one's feet could swell while sitting that long of a time and I had a horrible time getting them back on. I knew I would never do that again.

We landed in New York City — I think it was La Guardia Airport — without seeing the Statue of Liberty or Ellis Island. To this day I still haven't seen those two sights in person and for some reason it is very important for me to see them. I have vowed that I will somehow see them before I die.

In New York City we had to go through customs. This was an extremely intimidating experience for me as nobody spoke any Dutch, and my English was extremely limited. I remember the customs' area was dark and dreary looking — not a very welcoming feeling. I was tired and worried about Marian since she was only one month old and experiencing so much in such a short time. But she seemed to be alright.

Going through customs was not a positive experience at all. My suitcases were practically emptied as the agent started digging around in my bags, and upset all the neat little piles my sister had made to get everything to fit in. When he was satisfied that I did not have whatever he was looking for he pushed the suitcases aside and told me that I could go on. I had to repack everything and keep an eye on Marian and my belongings. This wasn't an easy undertaking as we could only have two suitcases and a total of 44 lbs. It didn't look like a lot when my sister was putting everything in my two suitcases, because it seemed so easy for her. But I remember that I had a hard time getting all the things back in the suitcases.

I almost got into trouble because there were some matches in one of my suitcases that my friends had given to me to remember them by. There was a nice Dutch scene pictured on the cover of the box. I was somehow able to let customs know that I had no intent of burning up the plane and just wanted something to remember my friends by. After all, they were in my suitcase and not in my carry-on. I later found out that I could have had help going through customs because of my language barrier and having a tiny baby to care for. Unfortunately, nobody had told me that before. A lesson was learned and not easily forgotten. "Ask and thou shall receive."

The whole experience in New York City made me very uncomfortable. I made a vow right then and there that I would never fly into that airport again if I could possibly avoid it. So far, I have been able to keep that promise. Looking back though, I think that it really wasn't such a bad experience. Now that I'm a seasoned traveler and speak the language fluently, I know what's going on, what they want me to do, what they expect, and what I should expect in return. I'm sure it wasn't any worse than landing in Chicago, Los Angeles, Phoenix, Singapore, Frankfurt or any other major airport in which I have had to pass through customs. It was just too much for me to handle at that time. Nobody had really prepared me for it or told me what to expect. And, not speaking the language, surely didn't help either.

Once I was through customs, my cousin Frans met me at the gate. He worked for Air France and had promised to escort me to the plane that was to fly us to Chicago. I was very happy to see him because

I felt more and more overwhelmed and scared and was also getting very tired. After he put me on the right plane, and was sure that I was settled in, he had to go back to work. I had hoped that he could stay with me until the plane was ready for takeoff. I guess I wanted to stay with someone in my family who could speak Dutch, and who could be there for me. He was on his break, however, and needed to leave right away.

Shortly after Frans left, there was an announcement in English that we needed to leave the plane because of engine problems. I didn't understand much of what was being said, but when I saw all the other people leave with their belongings, I knew that we had to disembark. Since I didn't know where to go, I ran out into the lobby trying to find someone who would tell me where I could catch the next plane. I tried to follow some of the other people but couldn't keep up. There was nobody there to help me out, not even a stewardess or steward. I panicked and put Marian in a stranger's lap, and with the little English I knew, I was somehow able to get across to her, that I would be right back.

I don't think I was gone for more than a minute because realization set in that I could get lost in that big airport, and that I could lose Marian. So, I ran back, grabbed Marian and somehow made it to the right airplane after all. I was very naive in thinking that everyone in America was honest and nice and that nobody would hurt you. I was lucky that nothing happened to her. I still remember the lady's face when I dropped Marian in her lap. She looked very puzzled, and rightfully so.

The flight from New York City to Chicago seemed quite strange again. Nobody spoke Dutch on this plane, a sharp contrast to the flight that had brought me to New York. Now I was really on my own. What a scary feeling that was! The stewardess and crew were very nice, I'm sure, but there was just no way that we could communicate properly with one another, nor could I find anybody who could. Even though the actual flight was only about half as long as the one I had just taken, it seemed like a very long and lonesome flight. Our flight to Chicago had been delayed for more than an hour and I was flying in on a different plane, with a different flight number. Gary was waiting for me at O'Hare airport not knowing exactly what had happened to us. Finally, we were reunited, and he was there to do all the talking and to take charge. What a wonderful feeling not to have to worry about anything, to just sit back and let someone else take all the responsibility. He was very happy to see both of us, and now our little family was together again.

From Chicago we took a turboprop plane, the noisiest plane I have ever been on, to Waterloo, Iowa. As fate had it, we were sitting right by the engines, and we had to listen to the roar of the engines the whole time. We could not hear each other or Marian even when she cried. Finally, we arrived at our destination, and by that time I was really exhausted but also very excited. Marian and I had traveled at least 16 hours since we left home and with the time difference our bodies thought it was the middle of the night. I was ready for bed but wouldn't be able to sleep for several hours.

While I was getting ready to move to the States, and still living with my mom and dad, Gary was on his way to be discharged from the Air Force. He had quite a time returning from Germany. His C-54 military transport plane had broken down in New Jersey, so he had to stay overnight at Rhein-Main Air Base in Germany. Finally, the next day the plane arrived, and he was on his way back to the States. He flew through the night, stopped at Goose Bay Air Base in Labrador for fuel, and then continued for what he thought was his final destination for discharge, Dover Air Base in Delaware. That was not the case. Dover was fogged in, and the plane had to continue to Charleston Air Base in South Carolina, and another overnight stay because the plane had hydraulic problems. Time was running out. Was he ever going to get discharged before he had to meet me in Chicago?

The next day the plane flew back to Dover, but it was too late to go through the discharge process, so Gary had to wait another day. Fortunately, he talked with some airmen who had received their discharge that day. They said that he should be in line early in the morning as they only processed so many airmen each day. He got up at 3:00 A.M. and was one of the first in line at 5:00 A.M. All went well and he was on his way to Philadelphia to catch the plane to Chicago. There were mechanical troubles with that plane, so there was another delay. He finally got to Chicago and took a bus to Waterloo, Iowa, with only a day to spare before flying back to Chicago to meet me. As a result, Gary didn't have a chance to talk with some of his old friends and arrange a ride for us to and from the airport, so had to take a taxi to the Waterloo airport.

We were lucky to get a ride home with the president of Chamberlain Corporation, the company that Gary worked for. Gary knew him from before he entered the service and he happened to be sitting next to us on the plane. He gave us a ride to our destination — Gary's Aunt Ina's house. I don't remember what kind of a car took us to her house, but I know it must have been a big car as we all had plenty of room for our luggage and for us to sit comfortably.

I still have some very specific first impressions of Waterloo. The only other place I had ever seen so much snow was in Southern Germany and that had been in the mountains. I hadn't realized that we would be living in such a cold climate with so much snow. I guess I should have known that since Iowa is in the middle of a large continent, and I had learned in my geography lessons that those areas had "landklimaat" which meant they had very cold winters and hot summers. I liked snow so that part was exciting, but I didn't like cold weather. In the Netherlands, at least by the coast, the snow had usually all melted by the time we came out of school. Here it stayed on the ground for weeks.

The sizes of the houses and yards amazed me as well. Again, I thought everybody there must be rich because most of the houses were single-family homes, and had yards all around them, just like in the movies. In my little country, only rich people knew such luxury. I figured we were still in the rich part of town, and asked Gary when we would arrive at his Aunt Ina's house. To my surprise he said we were almost there. How could that be? I still hadn't seen any apartment buildings that go from corner to corner of the block and are several stories high. I thought she must be rich to be able to live in this kind of neighborhood. I soon found out, though, that there were very few apartment buildings in Waterloo, and that her house was not especially expensive.

We finally arrived at Aunt Ina's house, and I had my first meeting with one of Gary's family members. Aunt Ina, whom we just called Ina, was a very short woman, probably no more than five feet tall. Most people in the Netherlands are tall, and at five foot seven I was just average, or even below average. Now I was one of the taller women in the family. What a change!

Ina had agreed to let us stay at her home until we found a place of our own. She lived all alone and probably enjoyed having somebody around and welcomed us with open arms. When we arrived, she had a room all ready for us, and we got Marian situated in her little travel bed and ready for the night. The house had central heating, something I wasn't used to but learned to like really fast. How rich I felt, not having to go to bed in a cold bedroom, and to wake up in a warm house. The only problem was that Ina kept the temperature at 80 degrees, day and night, which was normal in the 1960s, but was too hot for me. I had a hard time breathing and feeling good in that temperature, but still appreciated her hospitality.

Ina was the reason that, to this day, I don't like soft marshmallows. She had a bag of marshmallows open in the cupboard and they were hard and chewy. I sure liked them that way. Eating Smores is not one of my favorite treats as the marshmallows get all soft and mushy and I always have liked chewier things to eat. At her house I was also introduced to basements. What a clever idea of making use of an otherwise useless space. In the winter one could hang up the wash to dry, and there was lots of space for a laundry room and even a huge freezer. I had never seen a freezer that big let alone in a private home. Later, I found out that some people even finished off the basement and made it even more useful as a recreation room.

With the help of a friend of Gary, we soon found an upstairs apartment in a large two-story house. It was very roomy and very comfortable, even by today's standards. We rented the apartment furnished since we didn't have any furniture, and no money to buy any right away. The living room looked out on the street and had big windows, something I really appreciated. I loved the streets in Waterloo as they were all wide and most of them had lots of trees. We had a large dining room, a big kitchen with a table in it to work on or eat at, and we had two bedrooms and a bathroom — plenty of room for a young couple. Again, I sure felt rich having that much space for just the three of us.

In the kitchen was a large refrigerator. I looked in awe at it and was trying to figure out what to put in it, and why it had to be so big. In the Netherlands we bought groceries every day, so we didn't need a big refrigerator, and most people I knew never had one while I was living there. It didn't take very long before I had it filled with all kinds of food. Most people went to the store only once a week — usually on Friday evening which was payday. Once again, I couldn't get over the size of all the packaged foods. The only other place I had seen such big pieces of meat, such as a roast beef, was at the base. But I didn't think the stores in a regular town would be that big. Didn't people go to the store every day and buy things fresh? And then there was so much choice for breakfast cereals. I eventually had to try them all. Even the produce was bigger. I sure would never have to go hungry living here. What a relief. And not to have to go from one store to another to get what you needed made a lot of sense to me. Besides that, it was fun to go grocery shopping with Gary and Marian and get what we all wanted.

The only thing Gary didn't like about the apartment was the bathroom. It was a large bathroom with an old-fashioned deep bathtub, sink, and toilet, but unfortunately, it had a Pepto-Bismol pink carpet in it, and the walls were painted pink. Gary didn't like the pink color as it reminded him of the Pepto-Bismol he had to take when he didn't feel good. The first thing Gary did was ask the landlord if he could repaint the bathroom. I didn't particularly like carpet in the bathroom either, but otherwise I was very happy to have such a spacious bathroom. What sometimes became a problem was that everything was in one room, so when someone was taking a bath and another wanted to use the toilet, they had to wait. In the Netherlands, the toilet and a small sink were in a separate room from the bath, which I thought made more sense. But I got used to that quickly enough.

Another nice thing was that we had a large back yard where Marian could be with me once the weather warmed up. I would set her on a blanket under one of the trees and she would play there with her toys. She also could wander all over the apartment when she started crawling, since we didn't have a play pen. There were no stairs to worry about because there was a door to the second-floor landing, and that door was always closed. We shared the garage with our downstairs neighbor, which was nice as the car was protected from the elements that way. We bought a 1953 Chevy for $125.00, and it served us well. I had never seen a big car like that before, but quickly got used to the roominess inside. We later drove it to Arizona and kept it there until we moved back to Iowa in 1968.

Fortunately, I really liked the apartment, and was hoping that we would stay there for quite a while. I had had such a turbulent year behind me that it would be nice to finally settle down. I wanted to get to know people, make friends in my new country, and lead a more relaxed life. I was hoping to get to know the people downstairs more. They were a young couple (Gary's friends from before the Air Force days), who had two small children. I was happy to hear that, as I would have somebody to talk to and share ideas with about how to take care of Marian and help me adjust to my new country.

There were so many things I needed to know. First, I needed to find a good pediatrician for Marian since she would have to get her shots and have regular check-ups. I was also looking for a good gynecologist because I needed to have my six-week check-up after Marian's birth.

Separately, I also wanted to learn about how people lived in the USA, was determined to learn the language and become Americanized as soon as possible. Nonetheless, I wanted to keep my Dutch heritage with its customs and be able to speak my own language whenever possible.

I soon found out that our downstairs' neighbors both worked full-time, and their children went to a babysitter. However, I was still easily able to get some of the much-needed information, as my neighbor worked for one of the best pediatricians in town and her OB/GYN was willing to see me at a very reasonable fee.

It seemed odd to me though why a mother of two young children, one of whom was a baby, was working. This was totally unheard of in the Netherlands. I soon learned that she wasn't the only one who worked while raising a family. When we went downtown to sign up for telephone service, I stepped into the building and much to my surprise saw rows of women, of all ages, behind their desks. Women working outside the home seemed to be the norm everywhere, and I found out that this was not only accepted but often necessary.

I was very lonesome in my big apartment all day. Yes, Marian needed care and attention, but she still slept a lot. The cleaning of the apartment certainly didn't take every minute of the day. It was too cold to go outside with a little one, and I didn't know anyone to visit with. Even though we had a telephone, I didn't use it much because I was too scared to answer it. I knew that I couldn't understand what a caller would want, and didn't know anyone who spoke my language or who would speak slowly enough so I could understand what they were talking about.

Our phone was on a party line, which was an interesting and new idea to me. We soon changed that to a private line, however, as Gary couldn't call me because of the busy people with whom we shared the line. They seemed to be on the phone every time Gary wanted to call me. I felt rich to have a phone though and was amazed that I could pick out one that wasn't black. I had a hard time deciding which color to choose. If my memory serves me right, I chose a yellow one.

Because I couldn't speak or understand English very well, I was not only afraid to answer the phone, but even more afraid to answer the door when someone knocked on it. You could hang up the phone much easier than looking somebody in the eye and then walk away without opening the door. The door into our apartment had lots of glass in it since it didn't open to the outside. So, both parties could see each other easily. One day, the inevitable happened; someone was at the door. I was amazed that someone would just walk right up the stairs and knock on our door! However, I soon learned that people had a right to come upstairs and try to sell us their wares. Even though I was rather scared, I was also very curious as to who could be there and why they would come and see me. I went to the door but made sure that it stayed locked. It was the Avon lady wanting to let me know that she was the new Avon representative in our area. She gave me a catalog and an order form. I opened the door just a crack, took the catalog, and quickly closed the door again. We didn't have Avon ladies where I came from, and I was totally confused about the whole situation. What the heck was an Avon lady? Nobody had told me about this way of selling merchandise.

Gary bought us a television as soon as we could afford one hoping that I would be able to watch some of the programs while simultaneously learning the language. It was a little black and white TV; color TVs were still very expensive then, but I still felt rich as my family didn't even have a television set when I left for the States. I could now watch shows like "I Love Lucy" and "Father Knows Best." I wanted to learn English as soon as possible and watched every show I could to pick up a word or phrase here and there.

I soon fell in love with those TV shows, including the soap operas. That was such a strange concept to me. Why they called it a "soap opera," I just couldn't figure out, but I did watch some of them regularly as well. Later, Gary explained to me that they were called soap operas because when they first started as radio shows they were sponsored by soap manufacturers.

When Gary came home from work, I would proudly tell him what I had learned and, if I remembered, ask him what a certain word meant.

He also got us a subscription to the Reader's Digest because he knew I loved to read, and he knew that short stories would be easier to read than a whole book. Also, the language in the Reader's Digest wasn't too complicated and I could underline words I didn't know and he would translate them, to the best of his ability, at a later date or I could look them up in my little dictionary. We also started doing "Word Power" every month and my vocabulary increased little by little. We still read the Reader's Digest monthly and do "Word Power" together. It's kind of fun to see how slowly, but surely, I improved my "word power" and sometimes I even come very close to having the same score as Gary.

Learning the language was not an easy task. One doesn't realize how many contradictions there are in English. Even the pronunciation is not consistent. For example: the "ea" in the word "read" is pronounced totally different than the "ea" in "steak" or the "ea" in the metal "lead." The "o" in the word "cow" is pronounced differently than the "o" in "row." I could go on and on; it was very frustrating at times as I thought I had learned a new word and would tell Gary what it was but he couldn't figure it out because of my mispronunciation. One time I asked Gary to pick me up some Bayer aspirin. In Dutch it is pronounced like "Buyer." He came home totally frustrated because he couldn't find any "Buyer" aspirin anywhere. Later, we would laugh about things like that. But how is a foreigner to know? Some words I still can't pronounce correctly; they are caller, collar and color. No matter how hard I try I can't pronounce them right. To this day when I want to straighten Gary's collar, he wants to know if I think he looks too pale.

I often made lots of mistakes and was quite embarrassed when I did and it made me feel very stupid. Sometimes people laughed at my mistakes and that made me feel even worse. I finally found out that most Americans only speak English and that they have a very hard time learning another language. I kept on practicing and reading and learning the language better and increasing my vocabulary. I wanted to be able to speak and understand it. I never ever expected anybody to learn Dutch just because I couldn't speak English. After all, I had been allowed to live in this country and I felt this was a big privilege. The least I could do was to learn the language of this wonderful country that had been so generous to let me live here. I never could understand why second and third generations still don't speak American or not even want to learn the language. I didn't want to forget Dutch though and spoke it as much as I could. Another reason I wanted to learn English was that I didn't like to have to wait for somebody to translate to me what had been said. That took time and I was impatient; I wanted to understand what was being said when it was said. Besides that, the translation is not always the same as the original; one can lose the essentials easily. So, while the weather was too cold to go outside, I spent a lot of time reading and watching the boob tube.

Soon we met some European people, and in a very interesting way. While I was in the hospital in Germany after Marian's birth, I read some Dutch magazines my mother had sent me. In one of those magazines there was a request by people who lived in Waterloo, Iowa, to send a postcard to their little girl, Angela, who had broken her arm. Angela had a brother named Michael. The father, Jan, was Dutch and the mother, Rosemarie, was German. They had met and married while living in Iowa. I couldn't believe it when I saw it. Here were people living in the town I was moving to that I had something in common with. I made sure I kept that magazine so that we could contact them after we were settled in Waterloo.

I had to get up my nerve to make that call as I had very little experience on the phone. But one day I called Rosemarie to introduce myself. It was so nice to meet someone from the old country. Jan still spoke Dutch which was especially nice since he could act as my interpreter as well as help me with my English. Rosemarie still spoke German which was helpful since I could at least converse with her in German if I didn't know something in English. I could also keep up my German that way. We became close friends before long and spent many evenings and days together.

That spring, Marian, Ina and I flew to Phoenix to visit Gary's parents. Ina paid for our trip because she didn't want to go alone and thought her brother and sister-in-law should meet their new granddaughter. Little Marian had her second trip by plane and wasn't even six months old. We spent a couple of weeks with Gary's parents, Ed and Isabel. I was happy to meet them but wished that Gary could have been with us for support. What happened if they didn't like me? What if I would say, not on purpose of course, something wrong? I remember that I had written something totally different than what I wanted to write before Gary and I were married. Gary had said that it would be nice if I could write his parents and tell them a little about myself. I was happy to do so but found it extremely hard to write an entire letter in English. By the time I was done I was tired and had to make an ending of sorts. So, I looked up in the dictionary the English word for "aanstaande schoondochter" which means daughter-in-law. Since it is not one word in Dutch I had to look up "schoondochter" which meant daughter-in-law and then I looked up "aanstaande." There were two translations for that one word one of which was "expecting" and the other one was "future". I didn't know which one to use so I signed off with "expecting daughter-in-law." They must have been wondering what was going on. I wanted to make sure I wouldn't make such mistakes again.

As soon as we got off the plane, I knew I would like Phoenix. It all looked so romantic; the mountains all around the valley, the palm trees growing high into the sky and then there were all the fruit trees. People had orange and grapefruit trees right in their yard, and some others even had swimming pools in their backyard. And then there were the sunsets; I had never seen such beautiful sunsets before. It also was nice and warm, and I was tired of the cold weather. I am an outdoors person and with temperatures below freezing one can't do too much outside with a little baby. Also, it was a big city with lots of things to do and see. I don't remember too much about that visit, but it must have gone well. They told us later by phone that they wished that we could live near them.

Soon we returned to Iowa and discovered that, during our absence, the snow had melted, and the grass had started to grow tall. The trees and bushes were blooming and some of them had the most beautiful flowers on them. In Den Haag you didn't see that many trees let alone all those beautiful flowering trees. Things were looking up as I now could go outside more and explore the area. Every day I borrowed a stroller from the people downstairs and began walking. They didn't need the stroller during the day as they were both at work. As long as it was dry and not too cold, I walked everywhere with Marian in the stroller. People were really amazed at how far I would walk, especially with a baby in the stroller, but I really got to know the neighborhood and the city that way. Marian got a lot of fresh air in her little lungs, and I had my exercise regularly; a win-win situation.

Gary and I made some new friends and I soon got invited to different kinds of house parties such as Tupperware. I also got invited to a party where I was supposed to bring a white elephant. I know I became quite worried as I had no idea where I would find a white elephant and when I did how could I get it to this person's house? As soon as I got home, I told Gary my predicament. He quickly explained to me that a white elephant is a gift that each guest brings to the party and then leaves with a different gift from someone else. I felt a lot more at ease then.

That spring Gary introduced me to something new again. He drove the three of us to an A & W Root Beer stand. I had never seen something like that. You drive your car into one of the many stalls outside a little building. I was totally confused. You mean you sit in your car, place your order and then somebody brings it to your car? Then you don't take it home and eat it at your dining room table? You stay in the car and either eat it sitting there or you chomp it down while driving back home or wherever? This seemed so barbaric to me. In the Netherlands, meals are a much more formal affair. One sits at a table which is nicely set with tablecloths and napkins and one doesn't pick up food with the fingers. So anyway, Gary wanted to surprise me and ordered a root beer for me. He wanted to be extra generous and got the largest size available. I took one sip and I hated it! He couldn't understand why I didn't like it but to me it tasted like medicine. I haven't found any of my European friends who like root beer. Another time he took us to a drive-in movie. What a strange idea. One goes by car to a big parking lot and puts a speaker in the window and sits in the car and watches a movie. It would have been okay if the bugs weren't so bad, and it wasn't so hot. I didn't care for that too much either. I wanted to see the movie in the comfort of a theater where you are dry and warm, not hot, and not bothered by bugs.

In May we went to Pella, Iowa, to see the tulips. Pella is a town that was founded in 1847 by Dutch people and could remind one of being in the Netherlands. That year had been colder than normal so when their tulip festival took place the tulips weren't blooming yet. Artificial tulips were lining the streets and the parks. I was extremely disappointed as I had waited so long to see real tulips again. But it was nice to see the Dutch heritage, hear the Dutch language and to be able to buy some of the Dutch foods and snacks I longed for.

It wasn't very long before all that grass created a lot of problems for me. I had never been around grass that much but remembered that, in the Netherlands, one nice day in spring, I went with my boyfriend, Simon, to friends out in the country. After having spent an afternoon sitting and walking on the grass my nose started running and my eyes became all swollen. I didn't seem to have too much trouble in Germany, so I had forgotten all about it. Now my allergies became very bad again and I was in tears all the time. First, I thought I had a cold but when it never went away and I constantly had a stuffy, runny nose, I knew it had to be allergies. Soon more people must have had the same problems because suddenly there were commercials for sinus problems on the TV. They kept saying "send your sinuses to Arizona" by taking a pill every day. Your problems would soon disappear. I wasn't much for taking pills but tried them anyway. They didn't help all that much so we started thinking about moving to Arizona.

Gary's parents had been trying to talk us in to moving to Phoenix ever since Marian and I had visited them. They wanted us all to be closer and see their granddaughter grow up. They assured Gary that there would be plenty of jobs for him, and that they would help us out as much as they could, if and when we would move to Phoenix. When my allergies became too much for me the decision was made. We would leave Iowa and make our next move, this time to Phoenix.

CHAPTER 11

We left Iowa on August 1, 1965, saying goodbye to our friends and swearing we would never move back to that cold state again. Again, I had to leave some of my things behind never to get them back. Gary had bought me a treadle sewing machine and I was so happy to have that so I could sew some clothes for Marian and me. Obviously, it wouldn't fit into our car and we didn't have the money to ship it to Arizona. Would I ever be able to keep the things I had received and wanted? Never, ever say, never! Leaving in August turned out to be a very bad decision. One shouldn't move to a desert climate at the hottest time of the year. But we were young and didn't think too much about that. We spent many hours on the road every day, traveling several hundred miles before stopping for the night. We must have been quite a sight. The only thing we shipped to Arizona was the washing machine we had bought just a few months before our move. The space between the front and the back seat was jammed with our belongings and we had more in the trunk and in a luggage rack on top of the car.

Because our car had no air conditioning, we got up very early in the morning to do a lot of the driving while it was still cool. Marian sat in her car seat in between us because that was the only place available. When she got tired of sitting in her seat, I would take her out of the seat and hold her on my lap. I could do this because there were no seat belt laws at that time. She enjoyed that a lot, as she could see more and move around a little more. She traveled well considering we were in the car for long periods of time, and she was not able to do any crawling or move around much. It was a little harder on her when it became really hot. She needed to have a lot more water and needed to have the perspiration wiped away almost constantly. We gave her a wet washcloth to suck on as well as ice cubes and she drank many bottles of water or juice. I cannot imagine making a trip like that again, but we didn't know any better then. We did make sure that we would be in a motel with air-conditioning sometime in the afternoon. At least then we could cool down and have a good night's rest before continuing our journey the next day.

The trip across America was almost overwhelming for me as well. I had never seen so much land with so few people or houses in it. I was thinking how crowded it was in the Netherlands and here was all this empty space. At times we drove almost two hours without seeing anyone else on the road or anywhere else. I couldn't help but wonder how we would survive if something were to happen to our car or to us. We didn't have any way of getting a hold of anyone as there were no cell phones in those days and we didn't have a CB radio either. Besides that, who would have heard us? Once in a while we would see a farmhouse far in the distance. Again, I was asking myself how those people were able to live with no neighbors nearby. It would definitely be too desolate for me; I needed people around me. The scenery was often very beautiful, and we thoroughly enjoyed looking at that and thinking about future trips we could take and explore those pretty areas some more. Other times the scenery was very boring. The roads were straight and nothing interesting to look at no matter which direction you looked. It seemed like those boring parts of the road would never end.

We were lucky and nothing went wrong with the car or with us until we came to the mountains in Arizona. Our poor old car did not like the steep mountains between Payson and Phoenix and the radiator boiled over. We were fortunate that we had brought five gallons of water along. After letting the car cool down some Gary poured some water over the radiator to cool it down some more and filled up the radiator. Soon we were on our way again. Luckily the final part of the trip was mostly downhill. By the time we made it to Phoenix all of us were very hot and exhausted. Ed and Isabel were waiting anxiously for our arrival. They lived in a nice little house that had two bedrooms, one bathroom, but no garage. A lot of houses in that area had carports shading the cars most of the time. There was no central air-conditioning in that house, but Ed had installed a cooler in one of the windows which helped cool down the house most of the time. The humidity was still very low in the 1960s and people complained when it was in the double digits. They also had a nice big backyard. I soon found out that Gary's dad had a green thumb as his yard looked very, very nice. There was a big grassy lawn which had to be reseeded twice a year. I guess there was no grass that would stay alive all year around. Reseeding the yard twice a year seemed like a lot of work, but it was well worth it. He also grew a variety of vegetables and fruits in his backyard; something I was still hoping to have someday. We played croquet on his nice lawn many times and Marian had a lovely place to play without having to worry about wandering off.

Ed and Isabel hadn't seen Gary since he went to Germany, and now all of us were finally together. They had bought a crib, a high-chair, and a stroller for Marian. This was great as we did not have any of these items, and no money to buy them. They told us not to worry about anything as we could stay with them as long as necessary. They were just so thrilled to have their son with them again and the new little granddaughter who had been born on their wedding anniversary. However, they did tell us almost right away that they were happy to see us and would help in any way they could, but they wouldn't take care of Marian overnight. It wouldn't be fair to ask them to do so as Isabel had a full-time job and needed her rest. They also assured us again that it would not be too hard for Gary to find a job.

As it turned out, there were lots of jobs available, but not necessarily in Gary's field. We also found out that the pay was much less than he had received in Iowa. Since a lot of people wanted to move to Arizona, employers could pay their employees less. After all, if Gary did not want the job someone else would soon show up and be happy to take it. We then wondered if it the cost of living was cheaper in Arizona. It wasn't. It took several weeks before Gary found and accepted a job. He only stayed there one morning and quit. He didn't like the conditions and knew he wasn't going to be able to adjust to them as he was told he had to do with what was there.

He soon found another job which was closer to home and that was better as well. After he started working, we found a duplex and moved in over the weekend. Our happiness was short-lived as we ended up living there only one week. I hadn't even unpacked most of the things we had even though there wasn't that much to unpack. The duplex we had rented was single-story. We had purposely picked that one thinking it would be quieter that way as nobody would be living above us to make noise. Soon we heard footsteps on the roof and found out that some of the neighbor kids were using the roof as their playground as well as running and screaming through our yard. Their parents didn't seem to care and neither did the landlord. So, we had to look for another place to live. I soon found out that moving was going to be a regular thing for us. I became very good at packing and unpacking. We moved 11 times in 16 years, and finally lived in one house 15 years.

The next apartment was better and not too far away from Ed and Isabel. I could walk to their house if it wasn't too hot. It faced a big parking lot that belonged to a church so during the week there was room for children to play. It was a four-unit apartment, all in a row, and no upstairs neighbors. The landlord and his wife lived in the end apartment making sure everything was quiet and people respected each other. The people next door had a little girl who was a little older than Marian. We spent quite a bit of time together. I could ask questions about customs and the language.

Living in Arizona brought lots of new experiences again. In Iowa people had basements in which they stored their washing machines and dryers and other things. In Arizona there were no basements. Because there was no room in the house for the washer and dryer, they stood outside against the house under the overhang. I kept wondering if I would wake up one morning and would find that they were gone. Or would somebody come and use them while we were away? And what happened to the machines when it rained? Wouldn't they get shorted out? Even in the desert it does rain occasionally, and when it does, it pours. I was assured that all would be well. This was the way it was and there was nothing we could do about it.

In Phoenix you really didn't need a dryer unless there was a dust storm. We never knew when that would happen, though. If the wash was hanging outside during a dust storm, it would have to be rewashed. But if there were no dust storms and if the temperature was right, you could hang your wash outside and take it in almost by the time you were done hanging up the last piece of clothing. So, to make sure that your wash wouldn't get dirty because of a dust storm you stayed home while it was drying. If an unexpected dust storm would come up, you could quickly take in the wash.

Even though it was very hot in Phoenix, it was quite bearable with some planning. Since the humidity was so low and you made sure you stayed inside during the hottest hours of the day, one could live with the temperature just fine, even without an air-conditioner or a cooler. Marian and I would take naps during the hot time of the day, and I am sure Gary was comfortable at work. Traveling by car was a different situation. We soon found out that having air-conditioning in your car was not a luxury when driving in town or in the desert. It wasn't so bad if you kept on driving with the windows open, but waiting at stoplights was the real killer. Our car didn't have air-conditioning, so we quickly learned to always carry plenty of water and juices with us even if we just went for a few blocks, a precaution just in case something happened while en route. On longer trips we carried a five-gallon jug of water — something Ed had told us to do, and it seemed to make lots of sense.

From the beginning, Marian learned the advantages of drive-in restaurants. She quickly learned the signs of all the different drive-ins.

Her favorite one was Jack-In-The-Box. If we had to run errands across town, we had to stop several times at a Jack-In-The-Box and get her a drink. The poor girl could not take the heat at all.

I soon learned about Halloween and the funny costumes the children wear on that evening. It was so cute to see the children come to the door in their costumes, with their sacks ready to be filled with candies. I had never heard of that tradition before.

Shortly after that I celebrated my first Thanksgiving. My mother-in-law invited us for the traditional Thanksgiving dinner, and I learned all about the pilgrims and why we ate the food we did. This was only the second time in my life that I had eaten turkey; the other time was at Christmas in the Netherlands when Gary brought a big turkey he had bought on base.

Then on December 6, "Sinterklaas" came and went. I sure missed the Dutch tradition of Sinterklaas and tried to tell the American children the story of Sinterklaas and what that celebration had meant for me.

Saint Nicholas (Sinterklaas), a Bishop in Turkey, became well-known in the 4th Century for his charity, his love for children, and his concern for sailors and ships. He supposedly died on December 6, 343 A.D., and his feast day, the Celebration of Sinterklaas, is celebrated on that date.

Sinterklaas wears a long, red robe, a bishop's miter and carries a golden shepherd's staff while Zwarte Piet's clothes are in the Renaissance fashion of puffed velvet breeches and a jacket in bright colors and a flat, floppy hat. He has bright red lips and wears a large golden earring in each ear. Legend says Sinterklaas and Zwarte Piet traveled from their home in Spain across Europe helping the poor and bringing food to the children. Zwarte Piet was a Turkish orphan traveling as Sinterklaas's helper, and not a black slave, as some people believe. The legend of Sinterklaas on his white horse Schimmel with his helper Zwarte Piet became a tradition to celebrate the feast day on December 6th.

In the past Sinterklaas, Zwarte Piet and Schimmel sailed to the Netherlands on a steam ship from Spain. They left in mid-November and arrived on December 5th. Sinterklaas, Schimmel and Zwarte Piet jumped from roof to roof to all the houses and Zwarte Piet would slide up and down chimneys, leaving small gifts and treats like pepernoten, chocolate letters, marzipan figures, and fruit in wooden shoes left by the fireplace. Children filled their shoes with hay and carrots for Schimmel. Zwarte Piet carried a birch switch to punish children who had behaved badly and would put naughty children in his sack or leave them a lump of coal in their shoes instead of treats.

When I was growing up, Sinterklaas would arrive sometime in the middle of November and ride Schimmel through the streets of all the towns while Zwarte Piet would walk next to them carrying his sack over his shoulder. In his sack he had pepernoten and small candies which he would throw into the crowd of children and parents waiting anxiously for their arrival. The children would pick up the treats from the street and eat them then and later. These were unwrapped treats, but nobody seemed to worry about letting the children eat them like that. Having seen Sinterklaas and Zwarte Piet was the sign that we could put our shoes by the wood burning stove in the living room whenever our parents allowed us to do so. I don't remember leaving anything in the shoes, but we always found some small treat in the shoe. I don't remember ever getting a lump of coal in my shoe. Of course, we could hardly wait for December 6 when we would get our presents. As soon as Sinterklaas and Zwarte Piet had delivered all the presents they would all go back to Spain where Zwarte Piet was in charge of keeping track who was good and who wasn't.

We would buy or make presents and wrap them up in various ways so that people had absolutely no idea what could possibly be in the package. Sometimes the package had somebody's name on it but when the first wrapping was removed there was somebody else's name on the package. A package could change hands many times, and often did, keeping everybody in suspense as to who would finally be receiving the gift.

We also made "gedichten" which were poems that were based on the person who received the gift. You could write most anything in the poem; if you were good at writing poems you made a long poem and wrote some of the nice things about that person or something funny that you remembered he or she did. If you weren't good at writing poems, you could get by with no poem inside the package, or you could go to somebody in one of the department stores who would write one for you.

Of course, in America, instead of "Sinterklaas" there is a jolly old man with a big white beard and a big belly named Santa Claus. He comes on Christmas Eve and has only reindeer to help him get to the houses where he has to deliver the presents by going down the chimney. Since we didn't have a fireplace and therefore no chimney, how was he going to get the presents to us, Marian wondered? It was hard to get in the mood for Christmas when we were living in Arizona. After all, the sun was shining bright most every day in December and the weather was warm enough for us to go without coats. And there was no snow, sleet or fog. For me to get into the Christmas spirit the weather had to be cold and dreary. It still is hard for me to get in the Christmas mood in Phoenix and to see Santa in his bright red suit standing or walking around in the streets without any snow around.

I hadn't spoken to my family since I moved to the States because calling was very expensive. If my memory serves me right, it was something like $9.00 per minute. Gary told me that I could call my family on Christmas but could only talk for three minutes; that was all we could afford on his wages. He had to work one whole day for me to make that short call. I was really looking forward to hearing their voices again and was already preparing what I could say in such a short time. We still didn't have a phone by then, but the manager told me that I could use her phone. There was no direct dialing for overseas calls yet, so we had to call the operator ahead of time and tell her what number we wanted, on what day and what time and then we had to hang up. When she had reached the right party, she would call back and then we could talk. It was all very confusing, but it did work. When the time came for me to talk to them, I noticed that I could barely talk loud enough for them to hear me. I had my first bout of laryngitis, perhaps due to nervousness, which went away not long after I hung up. But we were able to exchange some news; those three minutes went by very fast though.

Next was my first New Year's Eve. How different that was again. In the Netherlands we eat "oliebollen" and "appelflappen" which are deep fried treats one only eats during that time of year. The person who makes those treats spends all day making big piles of them. On New Year's Eve everybody stays up until midnight eating all the different kinds of treats; then everyone goes outside at midnight and sets off fireworks in the streets.

I had invited Gary's parents and a few friends over to spend New Year's Eve with us. And I had spent most of the day making those special treats. I was very proud as they turned out so good. I soon found out though, that people liked them a lot but could only eat one or two and then they were full. They kept saying "they are so rich". I sure couldn't understand how a deep-fried treat could be rich as I associated rich with having lots of money. So, I learned another meaning for the word rich.

After everybody left, Gary and I reminisced about the past year. We had had another whirlwind of a year. I had immigrated to America and lived with his aunt; then we had moved into our first apartment in Iowa. Six months later we moved again, but now across the country to another state. We first lived with Gary's parents, and then moved into an apartment only to be packing up and moving again. Would this become a normal thing for us?

In Arizona I was first introduced to Country and Western music. I sure liked it from the first day I heard it. I liked the music part, but also the songs were sung slowly and clearly enough for me to understand what they were singing. Johnny Cash, Hank Williams, and Jim Reeves were some of my favorite performers. More would be added to my list later. We soon bought some of their records so I could listen to them any time I wanted to. Listening to country music helped my English except that the grammar isn't always correct. I found that out when I started saying things like: "He don't do that," instead of "He doesn't do that."

Coming from the Netherlands with an excellent public transportation system, I could not adjust to the bus system in Arizona. It was quite complicated, and to go a relatively short distance often required long travel time. And waiting in the hot sun for the bus was no fun either, especially with an infant.

We decided that I had to learn to drive a car. At the same time, I was scared that I would never be able to do it. I remembered my driving lessons in The Hague and the scary experience associated with it. Then there was the language barrier. But most of all, there was the thought of maneuvering that big car around corners and on the freeway. But the thought of sitting in the house or waiting for others to drive me whenever I wanted to go someplace made me overcome any fears of failure. In the Netherlands I had been independent and could go any place and at almost any time I wanted either by bus, bicycle, or train.

Gary offered to teach me how to drive. What a wonderful idea to have somebody who is not an instructor teach you how to drive! In the Netherlands you had to learn from an instructor. After a few attempts it became obvious that he should give that job to somebody else. We always seemed to end up in a big fight because I just had such a hard time learning to shift at the right time. We contacted a driving school so that the instructor could deal with my mistakes. After all, isn't that what he gets paid for? I was quickly told that I had to pass my written test first before I could take any lessons. My English was still not very good, but I could communicate in very simple ways and Gary was always there to help. I studied and studied, and it wasn't too long before I thought I might be ready to take the test. There was only one thing I didn't understand so I asked my mother-in-law if she could explain to me why somebody had to go to jail for manslaughter. I had learned the word laughter, but not yet the word slaughter, so I divided the word up at the wrong place and asked her about "man's laughter." Everyone had a good laugh about that and explained to me the real meaning! I had to get used to being laughed at because I made plenty of mistakes in grammar as well as in pronunciation. It bothered me a lot to be laughed at and it didn't help my feeling of self-worth. Again, I was reminded by Gary and some other friends that most Americans speak only one language and I had quite a bit of knowledge of three and was working on the fourth.

Anyway, I passed my written test right away and felt rather proud. After one lesson with the instructor of the driving school, we were informed that it would take at least twenty lessons before I would be able to try out for my driver's test. We calculated how much that would cost and quickly realized that there was no way we could afford that. My heart sank as I could only foresee years of me waiting for a license. One time while visiting Bob and Penny I told them my predicament. Penny, who is also a very independent woman, could understand my predicament and offered to teach me to drive if we would come to her house. She and Bob lived in Tempe and were students at Arizona State University. We lived in Sunnyslope, so it was a long drive but still cheaper than taking the lessons from an instructor. Penny was very patient, and it didn't take me as many lessons with her as the instructor of the driving school had predicted. Could it be that they set a prede-termined amount for everyone to have more cash flow?

Anyway, the big day finally came for to me to take my driving test. Ed drove me to the Department of Transportation. He could have let me drive as I had my driver's permit, but he wouldn't. I remember that day very well. It was very cloudy, and I was not used to driving under those conditions. With the very thick accent that I still had at that time, I told the examiner, while walking to the car, that I didn't know if I could take the test that time. He asked me why that might be. I told him that I had never driven when it was cloudy; everything looked so much different. He must have wondered what kind of kook I was. I wanted him to tell me that I should come back when it was sunny, so I wouldn't have to take the test that day. I was worried that I wouldn't pass and was looking for an excuse to not take the test. However, he quickly reassured me that I would do just fine, and we drove off. I passed the first time and was rather surprised that the test was not harder. I didn't even have to parallel park which I was very happy about, as I didn't feel very comfortable doing that with our 1953 Chevy. To me it felt like driving a big old tank. I preferred to walk a couple of blocks than try to squeeze that big boat in between two other cars.

However, I did have to park diagonally which wasn't all that easy for me either. There was no power steering in my car and turning the wheel sharp was not all that easy for me. My first attempt wasn't very good, and I hit the bumper of the car next to me. I just barely touched my bumper against his, as I was going very slow, and was able to stop immediately. The examiner asked me if I had hit the other car. I rolled down my window, stretched my neck out and took a good look. I said that I had hit the car, and he asked if there was damage to the other person's car. I looked closer but was able to say that everything looked fine. He said to back up and try again. This time I did okay and after I turned off the engine, he got out of the car, and I remained seated. I thought I had flunked for sure and wouldn't get my license. He asked me why I wasn't getting out of the car, and said I needed to get my picture taken and pick up my driver's license. I was shocked! I said, "you mean I passed?" He said that I had done just fine and only needed some more experience. Ed had watched all this from the window of the driver's license bureau and couldn't believe that I had passed. He wouldn't let me drive back to his house. It was my car, and I finally had my own driver's license, and I still had to be driven home. He didn't have much confidence in me, I guess.

Obtaining my driver's license, especially after only one try, was another rung up the ladder of success for me believing that I could do something, that maybe I was not really all that dumb. Even the Queen of the Netherlands didn't get her license on the first try! In fact, I didn't know anyone in the Netherlands who had a driver's license at my age. Granted, driving in Arizona was a lot easier than driving in the Netherlands, but that didn't stop me from feeling good about what I had just done. I was so proud when I had that driver's license in my hand; I just kept looking at it and thinking about it. Now I wanted to do nothing but drive and explore the area. There was so much to see and find out about. And, after all, didn't I need more experience?

I felt like a queen driving everywhere. I didn't care that we had a car that was 13 years old — I had wheels. I took Gary to work each day so I could have the car. Marian and I drove all over the place, even though we had to make frequent stops to get her a drink or to change her diaper. I had to learn my way around always paying attention to where I was going and where I had been. I hardly ever used a map.

Those were the turbulent 60s with the slogan "Love it or Leave it." I was constantly asked if I loved America better than the Netherlands, and wasn't I thrilled to death to be living here rather than in the Netherlands? How could I know? I had only lived in America for a year or so and had to deal with so many different things and customs. I was still getting used to this wonderful country, but certainly didn't want to say bad things about my country. Understandably, I missed my little country with its quaint customs, as well as my family and friends. I was totally confused.

Over the years I have learned that there is no perfect country, but that America is, at least for me, the only country to live in. As much as I miss certain things in the Netherlands, and, of course, my family, I wouldn't go back to the Netherlands for any reason. Anyway, when people asked me if I loved America better than the Netherlands, and I didn't reply positively they said: "why don't you go back from where you came?" They just didn't understand all the emotions that I had to deal with.

When I had lived long enough in America to become a citizen, I was expected to give up my Dutch citizenship right away. As I was still quite confused about all this, and I remained Dutch which made some of them extremely upset. Finally, I was able to come up with an answer so they would leave me alone. When they asked me why I didn't become an American citizen, I would ask them if they would give up their citizenship if they moved to a country outside of the U.S.

They said they wouldn't do that. So, I asked them why they expected me to give up my citizenship. I have wanted to become an American citizen at different points in my life. Initially I couldn't become a citizen without giving up my Dutch citizenship, either because America wanted me to give up my Dutch passport or the Netherlands wanted me to do so. Now, I want to become an American citizen, but need to save up some money to do so. And I look forward to doing so as soon as I can afford it. The problem is that they keep raising the fee and it is getting more and more expensive.

Gary's job was steady, but he was making less money than he had made in Iowa. I wanted to help so we could do a few extra things once in a while, like going to a movie, eating out or doing some sightseeing. There were so many beautiful parts of Arizona I wanted to see. We couldn't do anything on the wages he was making. So, I started looking around for ways to earn some extra money. My English wasn't really that good yet, but I figured I could do something to help financially. Now that I had a driver's license, I shouldn't have much difficulty finding a job. I didn't have to limit my job search to an area close enough to home for me to walk back and forth.

I applied at some of the local grocery stores and at the dime store. The manager at the dime store was very impressed with my math knowledge. To me it was just some simple calculations just like I had learned in the drills at school. However, he did not hire me. I was heartbroken but knew something would come along. Then I applied for a blue-collar job at Motorola. This wasn't an easy decision for me to make, as my parents had given me the message that it was below our status to work in a factory unless it was a white-collar job. But Motorola was known for good wages and benefits, so I applied anyway.

I really didn't think I would get the job because of my lack of proficiency in English, but I went through their testing programs and interviews anyway. This was my first experience with multiple choice tests. I did very well with all the tests, and to my surprise I did also quite well in English. I think I scored in the 90s. One of the few words I hadn't heard before was the word "tyke" and I made sure I remembered it until I got home to look it up.

After my final interview, it was decided that I would be getting the job and would start in a couple of weeks. They would notify me what shift I would be working and in which department I would work. I was so excited and looking forward to having a job and able to help financially. We didn't have a phone because we still couldn't afford one, so they agreed to send me a letter with all the details and the exact starting date. I didn't hear anything for three weeks and became quite upset. After all, hadn't he promised to let me know in two weeks? I wanted to work so badly and every day that I didn't work seemed like forever. I decided to write the interviewer and tell him what I thought. I explained that we keep our promise in the Netherlands, and when we say "two weeks" we mean two weeks. My letter was probably a bit harsh, and I didn't hear from him for another two weeks.

But finally, the big day came, and I started working. I had my very first job in the United States and I drove there all by myself. I had come a long way already. We had decided that I would work the second shift. That way I could be home with Marian through lunch and naptime, and Gary would be home shortly after I left. Marian would be with a sitter for an hour or less, and knowing this made it easier for me to drive back and forth to work. I didn't really like driving home in the dark through empty streets, but I felt confident that nothing would happen. It was still relatively safe to do so.

My job consisted of testing solenoids on a voltage tester. It was very tedious work and rather boring, but I was earning money and I got to drive the car every day and meet some new people. I made more money than Gary did so that helped tremendously. I also learned some new words that made Gary proud of me, and some he wished I had never heard. I soon found out that I had to be very careful about what I repeated.

Gary doesn't think it's necessary to say things in a vulgar way, and some of the words I brought home were anything but ladylike. This was very confusing to me as I didn't know what a good word to learn was and what was not. One time he had enough of what came out of my mouth and told me he was going to wash out my mouth with soap if I wouldn't stop. This behavior shocked me as Gary is such a gentle person. He was just kidding, but I finally realized how much I was offending him with my newly learned words.

Since we lived quite far from Motorola, we started looking for a different place to live. Again, our friends Bob and Penny came through. They lived in Tempe and knew of a house that was for rent in the same block as their house. Now we not only had a whole house to live in but already had some friends to visit with. Looking back, it was a very small two-bedroom house, but it had a small front yard and a little fenced-in back yard. Marian could play outside in the back yard and she would be safe. Our house, like so many other houses in the Phoenix area, had concrete floors that were just painted over and then waxed to look nice. They were easy to keep clean and cool to walk on in the summer.

I was learning more and more English, became a better driver, and picked up some bad habits from other people. Since I often didn't know what certain words really meant, I was proud to use them or say them. One time I was driving home from work, and somebody cut me off. I was quite upset that somebody would do that and showed him my middle finger. I had seen other people do it and didn't know what it meant but thought I would use that newly acquired custom. Well, this guy didn't like that at all and started following me as soon as he could get behind me again. I was scared as it was a rather remote road and in the middle of the night. I was wondering what I had done that he would do that. He certainly didn't look happy. He followed me all the way home but kept on driving after I pulled into our driveway. I was scared and told Gary what had happened. He quickly explained what I had done, and I assured him that I would never do that again. I was lucky that nothing happened to me. To make sure it wouldn't happen again, Gary called the police who came out and wrote a report. The next night after I came home from work, I noticed a car sitting in front of our house. I thought it might be that guy who had followed me, so I didn't pull into the driveway but drove around the block one more time. The car was still there so I drove into the driveway and parked my car and quickly went inside. Just as I was telling Gary what happened the doorbell rang. It was the policeman checking up on me to see if I was okay. He had been sitting in an unmarked car in front of our house.

We had a lot of problems with mosquitoes while living in that little house. This was caused by the front yard irrigation. Irrigation was another new concept for me. I had noticed that the front yard was sunken and had a couple of funny, round things coming out of the ground. I soon found out what their purpose was. One morning I woke up and the whole front yard was flooded. Marian thought that was nice, having a pool in her front yard. She played in it under close supervision from me, and she enjoyed it very much. Of course, all that water sitting there was a breeding place for mosquitoes. Soon thereafter we had an infestation of them all over the house, even with our screen windows and doors. Where did they come in? The only place that they might have come from was in the evaporative cooler. And sure enough, that was the problem. Gary climbed on the roof to see what he could do, if anything. There wasn't a whole lot to be done so we just learned to live with it.

Another time, after our yard was flooded again, I wanted to go out of the front door to let Marian play in the "pool." To my surprise the whole slab, and the wall on the front of the house was covered with snails. I couldn't believe my eyes; I had never seen anything like this before. I quickly closed the door and told Gary who assured me that everything was okay and that they would not do us any harm. I didn't use the front door until the snails were gone.

One day I was getting ready for work when I heard a scream. I had never heard Marian scream like that before, so I knew something was terribly wrong. I ran to her room, and she was standing and crying and holding her arm up toward me. Her hand was hanging down right above the elbow. She had fallen off her hobbyhorse and slammed her arm against the wall. Her arm was clearly broken.

Because I didn't have a phone, I ran next door holding Marian in my arms. My friend Leslie took one look at the arm and confirmed my suspicions. She drove Marian and me to the doctor's office. My pediatrician told me that it would be much better if we would take Marian to the hospital and have one of the specialists take care of Marian's arm. He didn't feel comfortable taking care of this kind of break.

I was a nervous wreck, as most mothers would be, and felt guilty. After all, if I hadn't left her alone while getting ready for work, she might not have broken her arm. The orthopedic surgeon took x-rays and set the arm. He wanted Marian to stay in the hospital overnight to keep an eye on the swelling. She was only about two and a half years old and looked so small in that big hospital bed.

We weren't allowed to spend the night in her room and went home promising her that we would be back first thing in the morning. Neither one of us slept much that night and very early in the morning we quickly got dressed and drove over to the hospital. We lived in Tempe and the hospital was in Scottsdale — not exactly down the street. It seemed to take forever before we were in her room and didn't know what to expect. Was she crying, had she slept at all, was she still in a lot of pain? These were some of the questions that went through our minds as we walked up to her room. When we walked in, she met us with a big smile and said, "You can take this off, Mommy. It doesn't hurt anymore." We were so relieved to hear that she had slept well and apparently had no pain. She had made it through the night, much better than we had. We explained to her that she had to keep the cast on for a while longer to make sure that the arm would be strong again. The regular cast had to remain on for four weeks and then she got a splint that we could take off when she needed a bath, or during the three times a day she had to exercise her arm. The arm finally was completely healed after eight weeks.

A small trailer court, my first experience with mobile homes, separated Bob and Penny's house from our house. Those homes were attractive and very efficient and soon we had decided that we wanted one too. We had set our sights on a brand new one as we had planned to live in it for many years. Ours was twelve by sixty feet, one of the first ones of that length. It had two bedrooms, one bathroom, a nice size living room and a big kitchen with a dining area where we ate all our meals. How proud I was of our new home, but I had to deal again with my parents as they thought we lived like gypsies. In the Netherlands only gypsies live in mobile home parks, except that they don't have mobile homes and live in trailers.

My happiness was short-lived. We only lived in it for about six months when we decided that Arizona was too hot for us and that we weren't making enough money to afford air-conditioning in the car and in the house. Without air conditioning we just couldn't live in the mobile home anymore and Gary started looking for another job. He applied at Boeing Aircraft in the state of Washington, which I would have liked as we would have lived closer to the ocean. I sure missed living near a big body of water. He also applied at Chamberlain Manufacturing, the place he had worked before, after he was in the service. He had no trouble getting rehired there and started as soon as he had given the proper notice at his old job. He got a job offer at Boeing as well but somehow felt that his job in Iowa would be much more secure. This turned out to be the right decision, as later Boeing had a big layoff and he might have been one of the many people that got laid off.

Marian and I reluctantly stayed behind. I didn't really want to leave Arizona. I still loved the landscape and the climate and remembered the cold winters back in Iowa. I knew, however, that somehow, someday, we would have to move back to Arizona again; I just had to. But for now, it seemed best to move back to Iowa. Maybe Marian would fare better as well. She didn't like the heat and was not able to play outside much at all.

We had to sell our new mobile home, which almost broke my heart. I had never lived in such a beautiful home and did not know if we would ever get something that new and that nice again. We also had to sell our 1953 Chevy because I was seven months pregnant by then and Gary didn't think I should drive it back to Iowa by myself. Selling the car almost broke Marian's heart. She cried and cried when the new owners drove off with it. I was sad about it as well since it had been our first car in the States. It had brought us to Arizona and taken us on some wonderful sightseeing trips. I did feel good about being able to sell the mobile home and the car without Gary's assistance, though. It was another small step towards raising my self-esteem.

On one of the last days I worked at Motorola, Bobby Kennedy was shot. I still remember our supervisor coming up to us to bring us the news. Here was another prominent political figure shot and killed. I certainly didn't feel too good about that.

Then a big tornado hit and did a lot of damage in a town not too far from Waterloo, Iowa. Ed and Isabel used that as an added pressure to stop us from moving back to Iowa. They really didn't want us to leave either. They told me, "Just tell Gary you aren't coming. He'll come back." Unfortunately, we couldn't stay, and the time came for us to follow Gary. By that time, I was also eight months pregnant. The women in my department gave me a nice baby shower. I was really excited, as nobody had ever done anything like that for me. I received many beautiful gifts that came in very handy and were much appreciated. Before we could fly back to Iowa to be with Gary, we had to have a moving company come and take our belongings and truck them to Iowa. Marian was sad about that as most of her toys had to go in the truck and she wouldn't see them until the truck had delivered our possessions in Waterloo. Soon after that the day came that Marian and I flew to Iowa. I was surprised that I was allowed to fly that late during my pregnancy, but again I wasn't really all that big, so they probably didn't know how far along I was. I remember that part of the flight was very bumpy, and I sure didn't feel very good during that time. But soon we were united with Gary again and started life in Iowa for a second time.

CHAPTER 12

Gary met us at the airport in Waterloo and told us that we could stay with the mother of one of his high school friends until we found our own place. We soon found a nice duplex to live and were able to move into it just a couple of weeks later. It had three bedrooms and was generally much larger than any of the other houses or apartments we had occupied so far. We were a bit disappointed as it didn't have a garage and now our car would sit out in the rain and cold. Now I needed to learn what to do when the windshield was frosted up. We were happy to have that extra bedroom since we were going to have another baby very soon. This place was not furnished, but Chamberlain had moved all the furniture from the mobile home to Waterloo for us. All we needed to buy was a stove and refrigerator which we did with the money I got from Motorola when I quit. I had worked there less than two years and received about $850.00 from profit-sharing funds. How happy I was to have that money! With that money we bought the latest stove and refrigerator and for once I was the one who had the newest gadgets in my kitchen appliances: an icemaker in the refrigerator and a griddle on our gas stove. I sure miss that stove.

We had just barely moved into our new place when I woke up early in the morning on July 15 with labor pains. I had had some pains all weekend but now the pains were worse. When the time was right, I called my doctor who informed me that I would have to go to Allen Hospital if I wanted him to deliver my baby. He was scheduled to do surgery there at eight o'clock. Allen Hospital was clear across town, and I had hoped that I could go to St. Francis Hospital, which was only five blocks from our house. No such luck though.

Gary and I got dressed quickly and then got Marian dressed. On the way to the hospital, we dropped her off at a friend who had volunteered to take care of her while I was in the hospital and Gary was at work. Marian was excited because we were going to pick up her baby sister with whom she could play. I don't know who was more excited about the new arrival, Marian or Gary and I.

The car we drove was a VW Beetle which was very hard for me to get in and out of by the time I was due to deliver. Being so cramped and then having the labor pains made it extremely unpleasant. I tried to stay optimistic figuring we should be in the hospital soon. I was hoping we would not have the misfortune to have to wait for the train. This train was famous for being so long that one could sit for twenty to thirty minutes before it cleared the tracks. I became very worried as I knew that it would not be very long before our baby would be born. I even told Gary to drive faster, exceeding the speed limit, but he was too worried about getting a ticket. He wouldn't believe that under these circumstances the police would not give him a ticket. According to him that only happened in the movies. We arrived at the hospital at about 7:30 a.m., and Hans was born within forty-five minutes. It was the same hospital where Gary was born, and was just a few blocks from where Gary worked, so he wasn't too late getting to work that morning.

While being pregnant with Hans, I hadn't had any morning sickness and had gained about twenty-five pounds. I wasn't too concerned about the weight since I had lost that much when I delivered Marian. I wasn't so lucky this time and lost only ten pounds. Hans weighed in at eight pounds, six and a half ounces, and like his sister, had no wrinkles and lots of red hair. In fact, when the doctor showed him to me and told me that I had a son I could hardly believe how much he looked like Marian when she was just born.

Unlike Marian however, Hans was very colicky, and the first three months were a bear. He cried and screamed a lot and was happy only when he was held and rocked, or while riding in the car. It was good to have that extra bedroom, so Marian didn't have to listen to him crying. Since I never had that problem with Marian, and I really didn't have any family or close friends to help us out I felt very insecure and was worried that I was doing something wrong. Why else would a baby cry so much?

Once Hans got through the colicky stage, he was as happy as he could be and only cried when he was hungry. He had a big appetite and seemed to be so much hungrier than Marian ever was. In fact, he still woke up at 2 a.m. for a bottle when he was eighteen months old. By that time, he weighed 30 pounds and certainly didn't look like he was starving. The pediatrician told me that I should just let him cry when he wanted his early morning bottle because he didn't need it and was old enough to be sleeping through the night. We had to put up with a few nights of him crying for the bottle, but he soon figured out that he wasn't going to get anything. What a relief. Marian never seemed to want to eat that much and slept through the night after six or eight weeks.

Since we had leased the duplex and didn't want to rent another year, we started to look for a house to buy. At first, we didn't think we could afford to buy anything because we didn't have a down payment. But we found out that we didn't need one because we could finance it through the Veterans Administration with no money down. What a wonderful thing to do for people who had been in the service. Soon we found a little house we could afford and were able to realize the American dream and buy our first house. It was an old house built around 1906. It was rather small, but it was ours, even though the bank really owned it for many years. It was a story and a half with two bedrooms and a bathroom upstairs, and a living room, dining room, and kitchen downstairs. Off the kitchen was a pantry that had been added on at one time and had not been built properly so it was starting to sag a bit.

In the fall mice would come in to get out of the cold. I sure didn't like that, so every fall we would set a trap and soon no more mice would dare come and visit our house anymore. We also had a basement under the whole house, but since it was so old, it wasn't good for anything other than storing junk and the washer and dryer. Later, we had to put support posts in the basement as the center of the house had started to sag around the chimney and needed to be held up.

We had a fenced-in yard which I liked because Marian and Hans could play outside without me having to worry about them wandering off. The first year I planted some marigolds, and they all came up great. They had a lot of buds on them, and I was looking forward to lots and lots of marigolds lining up the back wall of the house. One day I went outside to see how the kids were doing when I noticed that there were no more buds on the marigolds nor were there any flowers. Somebody had picked off each and every bud. I soon found out who this somebody was, and I must say he was very good at making sure he got them all. After my initial disappointment I had to chuckle. Next year Hans was bigger, and he knew not to pick the buds so we had lots of marigolds. Looking back, the house was nothing special and in need of a lot of repairs. But I felt very proud to have something we could call our own.

In the back of the yard by the alley, we had an old garage. It was small and so dilapidated that Gary decided to build a new one once we were settled in and had some money saved up to buy the materials. I was so surprised that one could do that without going through all kinds of red tape. Sure, you had to get a building permit, but that was easy. Gary figured out how much lumber, nails, roofing, etc. he needed, bought the materials, and started pounding away. A good friend of ours, Harris, helped him build the garage and in a week a beautiful new one was built and had lights inside so we wouldn't be in the dark when we came home at night. I was so proud of Gary that he knew how to do that. I would later find out that he could build anything, wire anything, fix the plumbing, etc. He is very handy and can do almost anything we need or want to do. We have sure saved a lot of money over the years because of his talents.

Before we moved into our home, though, we made our first trip back to the Netherlands. Hans was only ten months old, and we had expected to take him along and show him to all the family there. But about a week before we were to leave, we changed our minds and decided to leave Hans with friends in Waterloo. The Petersen's lived just a couple of houses down the road from us and had two kids of their own. We had visited with them many times and Hans knew the family well. They were happy to take care of him while we were in Europe.

We really were in a quandary about this. We wanted to take Hans with us but thought that the trip would be too much for him. I remembered how hard it had been for Marian when she moved to the United States and Hans wasn't much older than she had been. In fact, when I moved to the States, she was only one month old and slept in her little bed hanging over my seat. With Hans it would be different as he was old enough to be crawling and he certainly wouldn't want to be penned up for that long. Also, we first had to drive from Waterloo to Detroit. To catch the plane that left in the late afternoon, we had to either leave early in the morning or leave the day before and spend a night in the motel. We didn't have the money or the extra day for that, so we left early in the morning on the day of our departure, parked the car with some people in Detroit, and then caught the plane to the Netherlands. The long drive to Detroit followed by the long flight across the Atlantic and then the drive to my parents' house was more than we wanted Hans to endure.

The Petersen's were very nice people, and since Marian and Hans had been with them many times, we thought he would be fine with them. Indeed, he was as far as the care was concerned, but he really missed us. They said that all they had to do is call him by his name and he would start crying. We vowed that we would never do that again. We would all go or either Gary or I would stay home with the children. But we didn't know any better at the time.

When we arrived in Amsterdam, we were welcomed by my family who was very anxious to see Hans. Everyone was so disappointed that he wasn't with us. Showing them pictures just didn't do it. We spent three weeks visiting friends and family and trying very hard to catch up with what had happened during the past four years. The whole trip turned out to be quite tiring, but enjoyable. One thing that surprised me very much was how much I struggled with my own language. I could understand it easily enough, but speaking it was more difficult.

I had heard that you could lose your own language if you didn't speak it for a long time, but I had never believed it. It was true though and I soon found myself looking for words. However, it didn't take too long before I was able to carry on a conversation again. I decided that I needed to speak Dutch more often once I returned to the United States to keep my language skills.

We flew home after promising that we would do better keeping in contact with each other. And my mother said she would start saving for a trip to Waterloo. We were looking forward to getting back in Waterloo and especially to see Hans again. We all missed him terribly. Would he recognize us? Would he be healthy? What could he do that he couldn't when we left? Those were some of the questions we were asking. Upon arrival in Waterloo, we quickly went to the Petersen's to pick up Hans. For a few minutes Hans didn't seem to recognize us but then, suddenly, he came to us and wanted to be with us all the time. While were gone he had started walking. He especially clung to me and followed me everywhere. He simply wouldn't let me out of his sight for several months. It was as if an invisible string held us together.

The Petersen's had lots of questions for us. How did I like my old country, had things changed, did I get to meet all my family and friends, and would I want to move back there again? I could honestly assure them that I was happy living where I was and had no plans to move back. My homesickness, which I had for a long time, was now gone. I had thought that time would stand still and that everything and everyone would be exactly like I left them. But of course, that wasn't the case. Not only had I changed, but people and places had changed as well. I felt so much better about living in the United States once we got back from the Netherlands. Even though I missed my family, friends, and certain things about the Netherlands, I was getting more and more used to living in the States and enjoyed being here. Overall, the trip to the Netherlands had done me a whole lot of good. It had taken me a long time to quit feeling torn about where to live as each country had some things I definitely didn't like and some things I definitely did like. There just isn't a perfect country, but I do believe I am in the best place in the world.

Shortly after we came back from our trip to the Netherlands, we moved into the house that we had bought before we left. I have many good memories of living there. We generally got along with most of the neighbors, made a lot of friends with neighbors as well as people Gary met through work, and did a lot of socializing. We also started taking square dance lessons which not only helped me become more familiar with the language but also gave us a chance to meet more people, a good way to exercise, and a fun and cheap way of entertainment.

I enjoyed staying home with the children and playing games with them or playing with them on the floor. I was making up for the childhood I had never had. I would take them to the park every opportunity I had. The park was only six blocks away and it didn't take Hans long to walk by himself to the park and back. I also did lots of baking cookies and cakes; they helped with that, and we all enjoyed licking the bowls and spoons.

When Marian went to kindergarten, I was alone with Hans and that was fun, too. He always wanted to have a good time and he loved to have visitors because then he would get tea and cookies. He liked the Dutch tea that my mother always sent me from the Netherlands. One time I was working around the house, and he was playing outside when suddenly the doorbell rang. I wasn't expecting anyone and figured it was another salesperson. By that time, I wasn't worried about answering the door for them. To my surprise it was Hans with one of our neighbor ladies. She told me that Hans had invited her to have tea with me. He had gone over to her house and told her that I wanted her to come over and have tea with us. I had done no such thing but found it so cute that I dropped what I was doing, and we all had tea together.

Sometime in 1970 my mom decided to come and visit me. I hadn't really expected her to come so soon as she had told me the year before that she would start saving up for the trip. She came alone and explained to me that my dad didn't want to make the long trip. I later found out that it was because he had cancer and was in no shape to travel that far. Anyway, she wanted to know if I could pick her up from Chicago. She didn't really realize how far it was for me to drive, but since she was alone and this was her first trip to America, she felt much more confident if I could pick her up in Chicago. This way she wouldn't have to change planes. I remember making the long trip all by myself and driving through Chicago to get to the airport. I quickly realized how much I had become Americanized to be driving that far to pick somebody up from the airport. Nobody would have done that in Europe, but they have such good public transportation that it doesn't make sense to not make use of that.

My mother wanted something to eat before we started back so, knowing we had a long trip ahead, we stopped at a Burger King to get a hamburger. We sat down to eat (I couldn't ask her to eat it in the car just yet) and the first thing she asked for was the silverware. I told her that we don't eat a hamburger with silverware, but she wouldn't budge, and I had to get her a fork and a knife. They were plastic of course and that was not too good either but better than nothing. She ate her hamburger like an open-faced sandwich having the hamburger patty on one half of the bun and the lettuce and tomato on the other one neatly cutting it up in bite size pieces and eating them with her fork. The French fries she cut up as well and put into her mouth with her fork. Once we were done eating, we got back into the car and drove back to Waterloo. We made it home safe and sound which was another boost for my self-esteem. Driving to Chicago and back without Gary's help was a huge step for me. I did have roadmaps from AAA and that helped a lot.

Our house reminded her of the houses in Indonesia because we had a front porch to sit on. I was able to show her some of the beautiful parts of Iowa as well as parts of Wisconsin. When we crossed the Mississippi, she was so excited as she had read about it in books. She wanted me to stop in the middle of the bridge so she could take a picture of the famous river. She was quite upset with me because I wouldn't stop until I told her that we were not allowed to do so. She still didn't like it and thought it was a stupid rule. It was a lot of fun to show her around; especially since we went to places, I had never been to myself. She was very pleased with all the things she had seen and done and she and I would make many more trips after that. Gary stayed home with the kids most of the time. This wasn't easy as he had to go to work, cook the meals and take care of the kids as well. He didn't seem to mind.

My younger brother came the following year and spent a couple of weeks with us. I showed him some of the sights I thought he might enjoy in Iowa as well as in Wisconsin. I soon found out that I wasn't the only Dutch person in Wisconsin. He and I went to House on the Rock and stood in line to go inside. In front of us stood a woman with a dress I didn't think was too nice, so I commented about it in Dutch to my brother. To our amazement she turned around and proceeded to tell us, in Dutch, what she thought of us. We both wish we could have become invisible or fall into a deep hole in the ground. Later, I found out that there were several cities in Wisconsin where first generation Dutch people lived.

CHAPTER 13

In the fall of 1971, I realized that it wouldn't be too long before Hans went to kindergarten. I wondered what I would do with my days in an empty house. I didn't like being alone all day. I felt very lonely and abandoned and not very useful when I was by myself. Gary and I had decided not to have any more children. We wanted to do a lot of traveling because both our families lived so far away. We also wanted to make sure that we had enough money to live and do the things we wanted to do.

I checked into becoming a nurse again but found out that nobody wanted to accept any of the credits and experience I had earned in the Netherlands. It would have been different if I had had my diploma and now, I was sorry I hadn't finished my schooling and become a registered nurse. I was told that basically I had to start all over. I was angry that all my knowledge and experience had been for nothing. At the same time, I was very much afraid that I wouldn't be able to complete the program here. First, there was the language problem and secondly, I still didn't think that I would be smart enough to do it. I kept hearing my mother's voice saying: "She isn't very smart." I was certain they wouldn't have the variety of programs to choose from like the ones in the Netherlands which would not permit me to select the easiest one available. I inquired about enrolling at Gates Business College in the secretarial program and was accepted without any problems.

It was a very small school and was in downtown Waterloo. I enrolled for the fall semester. I still remember the first day. I was excited to learn something new and yet worried about my ability to finish it. There were several new students waiting in the hallway and we started talking about our expectations and concerns. It wasn't long before one of the new students literally passed out and I was there to help her. My nursing skills came in handy after all. Once she was sitting up again and able to talk, I asked her what had happened. She said that she was so nervous that she just passed out. It seemed that she did that a lot when she was tense. I felt pretty good because I had never passed out no matter how nervous I had been.

Once she was back to normal and seated in a corner, I looked around and saw a row of students typing away very fast. It looked so easy — their fingers were just flying over the keys. But I just knew that it wouldn't be that easy for me. I had never played the piano or done anything else to have limber fingers. However, the whole program turned out to be simple for me, even the typing. I did better than most of the students in most of the subjects and was soon summoned into the office of the administrator of the school. I don't remember what her title was, but she wanted to talk to me. She explained to me that I had the capability and the character to advance even more; she thought I should become an executive secretary. I didn't know what the difference was between a secretary and an executive secretary. She explained to me that an executive secretary was a private secretary and took care of only one person where a regular secretary could be hired to do the work for several employers. It was supposed to be a step up, and I liked the idea of working for one person only.

I figured that it would be easier than trying to please several people at the same time. It also meant that I might do some traveling when my employer went to meetings elsewhere and that I would be required to dress better and wear make-up. That last thing was something I didn't do, don't like to do, and still don't do. The administrator said I would have to pluck my eyebrows and take a course in grooming and applying make-up. I wasn't too thrilled about that part but figured that it was part of the program and needed to be done.

The first semester went fine, and I made the honor roll. I felt proud about that but still thought it was no big deal. After all, if I could get those kinds of grades, it couldn't have been that hard. It must have been luck. The next semester wasn't much harder, and I was able to help others with their assignments, especially with math.

On May 9, 1972, I came home from school and Gary was waiting for me. This was very unusual as it was before lunch, and he never came home for lunch. I asked him what was up, why he was home so early. He explained that he had received a phone call at work that my dad was critically ill. I knew that my dad hadn't been well for a long time, but I didn't realize how ill he had been. It seems that my brother had tried to call me at home, and nobody answered, so he called Gary at work. We didn't have answering machines or cell phones in those days. We were told that my dad might not live much longer and that it would be a good idea if I went home right away. I had never made that many arrangements and decisions in such a short time before.

One major complication was that my passport had expired, and I couldn't leave the country without it. Gary called the Dutch consulate in Chicago and explained the situation. They were very helpful. Since I had to leave from Chicago anyway and my plane to the Netherlands wouldn't take off until later in the afternoon, they would take care of me first thing in the morning. All I needed to do was show up with my old passport, a couple of black-and-white pictures, and the fee and they would take care of everything right away.

We called a travel agent, explained our situation and got two tickets, one for me and one for Hans. Hans had never met his opa, and we had hoped that we wouldn't be too late for him to meet him yet. We charged the tickets on our MasterCard, the only credit card we had at the time. We had applied for an American Express card, but they turned us down saying Gary didn't make enough money to get one of their cards. We were so upset of the idea of them thinking that we wouldn't know how to use our credit card that we vowed we would never get one of their cards. We have had many "pre-approved" cards from them since then, but we just cut them up and throw them in the garbage. They didn't want us then, so we don't want them now! The travel agency didn't check with MasterCard to see if the amount was within our credit limit, and we really didn't think about it either. Our only concern was to get the tickets and to drive to Chicago. When the MasterCard bill arrived, we were notified that we were over our credit limit and we needed to pay the full balance right away. We borrowed the money from the credit union and paid off the MasterCard bill right away. The loan at the credit union was also paid off in just a few short months. Soon we got a letter from MasterCard stating that they now had increased our credit limit to exactly the amount we had borrowed before. How about that?

The next day we got up real early in the morning and left for Chicago. The Dutch Consulate was waiting for me and before I knew it, we were on our way to the airport. Everything went fine until I arrived at the ticket counter ready to leave. It seems that I should have brought my green card (my alien registration card) with me. They didn't want me to leave the country because I wouldn't be able to get back into the United States without that card. We explained the situation and they were still very hesitant about letting me board the plane. However, they really couldn't keep me either. They impressed on Gary the importance of sending me my green card right away so that I wouldn't have any problems getting back into the country.

The flight to Amsterdam was pleasant in that the plane wasn't full and I was able to lie across several seats in the middle row when I got tired. I let Hans run around in the plane and visit with people. At one point, after I hadn't seen him for quite a while, I began to get concerned. I knew that he couldn't be lost since the plane was relatively small, but I began to wonder where he was and what he was doing. He soon came back with a box of chocolates in his hand. It seems that the stewardess had taken him to see the pilot who had shown him all about the lights and knobs in the cockpit (imagine doing that now!). The pilot had given him the chocolates to share with his mommy.

Another time during the eight-hour flight, he came down the aisle and told me to come with him. He took me to a lady who was sitting by herself. He had talked with her and told her that his mommy was also by herself and maybe the two could sit together and talk. He always was trying to do things like that. He must have known by now that I didn't like being by myself. In this case I was tired and really didn't want to visit with anyone. I just wanted to sleep as much as I could since I hadn't slept well the night before. So, I talked briefly with the lady and told her that I was tired and maybe later we could talk.

We finally arrived at Schiphol where my younger brother and sister were waiting for me at the airport to take me to my parents' home in Den Haag. It was a 45-minute ride and when we were already in Den Haag about 15 minutes from home, my sister, who was seated in the front seat, kept asking my brother if he had already told me. He said "no". I wanted to know what he was supposed to have told me already. With a lot of hesitation, he said that my father had already died. In fact, he had died just shortly after we left the house on the way to Chicago, and they had tried to call us to let us know.

I never got to say good-bye to him. Gone was the man whom I really did not know, which became especially clear after I heard some of the things he had done before the war. It seems that he was so much different then: fun loving, energetic, and optimistic. The only person I ever knew was a man who didn't enjoy life and had a lot of anger inside him.

The funeral was a short service and then we all went to our house. Quite a few people showed up, mostly family and it was then that I learned more about my dad than in all the years that I had lived with him. People reminisced about the tricks he had played on people and some other things he had done in his life. A couple of the stories told that day stayed with me because they were so much out of character with the man I knew.

One story was about a time in Indonesia before the war. My parents gave one of their many parties for their friends and co-workers. My dad wanted to scare people when they stepped onto the porch. He had saved the body of a tiger he had killed and decided that he would put the dead tiger on the porch with a stick propped under its head. It looked quite alive — in fact so alive that he scared himself rather badly when he ran around the house and onto the porch, forgetting that it was there.

Another time he had the servants switch round silver cake decorations with something a little different. Normally the cake decorations are just little round sugar balls with a silver coating. The ones he had the servants use looked just like them but were laxative pills. Everyone who had a piece of cake had at least several pills on their slice. When the party was over everyone went home, driving on very winding roads, not suspecting anything. Supposedly some of the guests didn't make it home without having some problems.

There was laughing and giggling, but nothing inappropriate. It was good to see some of my family again, although it could have been better under different circumstances. I hadn't seen most of the people who were there for at least three years, others for seven years or longer.

After my dad's death, I experienced a lot of mixed emotions that I didn't understand. I was sad because I hadn't had a chance to say goodbye to him, and I felt guilty because I thought I should have known how sick he was. I asked myself, "Why didn't I know he was so ill? Why didn't anybody tell me?" I also felt sad because I had wanted to know the kind of person that everybody talked about at his funeral. I regretted not ever knowing the fun-loving guy, the person who liked to play tricks, and who had a sense of humor.

I was angry because I felt cheated. I could have had a father with whom I could have shared things, and whom I could have loved. I was angry because the war had changed this man so much that I never had the chance to be raised by the real person he had been at one time. I was also angry with myself that I had never been able to see the man he actually was, or maybe still was inside. I felt that maybe if I hadn't been so afraid to open up to him, we might have had a different relationship with each other.

And I was also relieved because I now didn't have to worry about what he was going to say or how he was going to react to what I said and did. Even after being married, I couldn't tell him everything that was going on in our life because I knew I would be criticized about it. I felt almost like a big brick had fallen off my chest. But I also felt guilty that I felt so relieved, and the conflict in my emotions confused me. I eventually acted indifferent to the rest of the world, and I distanced myself from the whole situation. When anyone asked me how I felt, I said I was happy he was dead because he didn't have to suffer anymore. Of course, I was glad of that because he had suffered a great deal with his ten-year bout with cancer. I was also happy that my mother could now come and go without being checked on all the time. She could write and receive letters without her mail being censored by my dad. At first, I didn't understand why she was pleased to be by herself, but later came to realize how much easier her life would be from then on. I was glad to have Hans with me so I could divert my attention and my emotions to him. He didn't understand at all what was going on as he had never met any of my family before, except for my mother and my younger brother, and he didn't really remember them. He wasn't even five years old when my dad died, and the only time he saw him was when he was in the casket. From then on, he referred to his Opa as the "man in the box". Marian remembered my dad as the only person she knew who could take out his teeth. She had seen him do that when she was four years old and that had made a big impression on her.

When we came back from the Netherlands, I caught up with the semester work I had missed at Gates College, but became bored with the whole program, as it all seemed too easy. I finished up that semester but decided not to continue any further and began to look for a job. I needed a bigger challenge and I wanted to start making some money.

I wanted to have a job that would permit me to be with my children when they needed me, at least most of the time.

When I had one of my yearly physicals, my doctor asked me what I was up to and what was happening in my life. I told him that I was looking for a part-time job and that I had nursing experience. He said that he was looking for a receptionist and asked if I might be interested in that job. I told him that I would think it over and let him know. The real reason I didn't accept right away was that he wanted me to work every other Saturday morning and the hours were more than I really wanted to work. I wouldn't exactly work full-time, but more than part-time, or about thirty hours a week. Since I didn't have anything else lined up, I did accept and started work soon afterwards. I enjoyed the work and meeting all the people while there. The pay wasn't great, but it gave me experience in filling out insurance claims and Medicare/Medicaid forms as well as doing EKGs, setting up appointments, and answering the phone.

I didn't particularly like paperwork, but it had to be done anyway. I knew that my passion was for people and helping them in whatever way I could. Doing EKGs was okay when the people were clean. However, we got a lot of people who worked at John Deere, and they usually came straight from work and smelled something dreadful.

It might seem that if one worked for a doctor, medical attention would be easy to get when needed. At least I thought it might be better than when I was working in the hospital in the Netherlands and had my problems with my appendix. However, this wasn't the case. One time I had a bad cold that turned into either pneumonia or bronchitis. I was coughing and hacking and looked like death warmed over. Even the patients suggested that I see a doctor. The doctor I worked for never suggested that something might be wrong and that I might need medical attention. Things got worse, and one morning I woke up with a fever of 104, which is high for me since my normal morning temperature is 96.8 degrees instead of 98.6. I decided to stay home that day and rest up. Gary called in sick for me, and I dragged my sick body around to get the children off to school. A couple of hours later, the phone rang, and Hans' teacher was on the line to let me know that Hans was sick and could I pick him up. I told her I couldn't possibly pick him up because I was too sick, and I passed out before I could hang up the phone. I had never passed out before and was lucky that I didn't hit the television or anything sharp as I was standing right by the TV. I don't know how long I was out, but when I came to, I hung up the phone and went back to bed. I was barely back to sleep when the doorbell rang. It was my neighbor wanting to know what had happened. The school had called her when I passed out and asked her to check on me. She suggested that I call the doctor and tell him what had happened and ask him to prescribe some medication. She offered to go to the drugstore and pick up the prescription. Soon I felt better again.

Even though I liked working for the doctor, there was some tension between the other girl and me. She had worked for the doctor longer than I and therefore had seniority. I realized that, and that would have been okay with me except she carried seniority a bit further than I thought she should. I also had become bored with the tasks I had learned and performed. I am still that way. I want to learn new things, but as soon as I know everything I need to know, or want to know, I want to do something different.

I started looking for a different job that paid better and where I would learn other tasks. I went to an employment agency and had them help me find a job. I still didn't think I would be able to find something on my own and was very happy to have somebody else look for me, even if it meant paying a fee for their services. To my surprise, it didn't take them very long and soon I was working for a photo lab where I learned to do accounts receivable on a computer. This was in 1973 when computers were still huge and frightening to most people, and certainly to me. The one I worked on was about the size of a large office desk. I pretended to be brave and learned as fast as I could. I had a very kind supervisor who told me that I was doing a great job, but of course I thought she was just saying it to make me happy and to keep me there. Later, I learned that she really was pleased with my work.

Soon I became bored with that job and wanted to do something different again. I decided to apply at Kelly Temporary Services. I figured it would suit me well because I could work when I wanted and could change jobs often. I really did enjoy those aspects of working for them but hadn't realized that they got a hefty commission for finding people like me. And I thought I should be paid more than I was getting for the work I was doing. I finally landed a job through Kelly Services at Kies Electric in Waterloo. I did accounts receivable, but this time the machine was a lot older and a lot noisier. They liked me and kept me as a temporary employee for several months, and then offered me a full-time job. I realized that I must have been a good employee because Kies Electric had to pay Kelly Services a fee for hiring me away from them. They must have thought I was worth the expense; I was really surprised to hear that. I stayed with them until we moved to Wisconsin in December of 1979.

In general, our years in Iowa were very happy. As I look back, I realize that I did a lot of growing. I always seemed to push myself to the limit with whatever I did, always learning or doing something new. At the same time, I had a tremendous yearning to have fun. It appeared to me that Americans continued to have more fun after they were married than married couples in the Netherlands. The message I had received from my parents was that there were certain things you didn't do once you were married. For example, you couldn't go roller skating down the street, you couldn't sit on the sidewalk and draw chalk pictures with your kids, a woman had to wear a skirt and not slacks even when riding a bike to get groceries, and so on. I don't know if that was my mother's opinion or expectation or if that was even true. But that is what I thought I had to do and be like. Once a person was married, he or she had to always behave like a prim and proper adult. I didn't want to behave like an adult, at least not that kind of adult. I could be very mature and do adult things, but I wasn't ready to give up the child inside me and my children have often asked me when I was going to behave like a grown-up person. I always told them that if growing up meant not doing the things I love to do, then I was never going to grow up. Now they don't ask, and even think it's great that they didn't grow up with a mom just like everybody else's mom.

I was the one who would take them to the park and to the pool. I must say that I sometimes embarrassed them in the pool. I would jump from the high diving board but would always pinch my nose shut and landed in the water kind of curled up. I was the one who would take them to Great America with their friends and would go on the rides with them. Other moms were too scared to go on the rides. I played tag and hide and seek and would ride my bike without holding on to the handlebars. I shot baskets in our driveway with them.

I always looked for more fun and different kinds of fun. One time I was at a mall in Waterloo, and they were giving a square dance demonstration. It looked like a tremendous amount of fun to me, and I talked Gary into taking square dancing lessons. Within a couple of weeks, we started lessons and went to as many dances as we could. We also went to regular dances with some our friends and were always the last ones to leave and the first ones on the dance floor. Afterwards we would have breakfast at two in the morning. I thought it was great and really enjoyed it all. I really was acting more like a teenager than somebody almost thirty, but I didn't care. One time I got excited at one of the dances because they were playing my favorite song. I ran to the dance floor and forgot that there were two steps to go down to reach the floor. I tripped and sprained my ankle. It hurt something terrible. I was told that a sprain hurts much more than a broken bone. I sure could believe that. But I always tried to look at the positive side of it which was that I hurt myself while I was having fun instead of when I was doing housework.

I was also getting more confidence and slowly became gutsier. One time, Tommy Cash, the brother of Johnny Cash, came to Second Base, my favorite dance place in Cedar Falls. I thought Johnny Cash was the greatest singer around but liked Tommy Cash as well. Unfortunately, I couldn't afford to see him perform. The tickets and babysitting fees were just not in the budget. I decided I had to see Tommy, no matter what, even if just for a minute. I drove out to Second Base, and there was his huge motor home sitting in the parking lot. I knocked on the door and a lady answered. I told her who I was, and that I was a great admirer of Johnny Cash as well as Tommy Cash and really wanted to see Tommy Cash that night. I explained the situation and asked if I could just get his autograph. I would be so excited to see him if only for a second. She told me to come inside and sit on the couch. I was in heaven that someone so famous would allow me to sit on his couch. Soon Tommy Cash came out with a big color picture of himself, and again I explained to him how much it would mean to me if I could hear him sing but that I would be happy just to have met him and to have his autographed picture. He signed the color picture of himself, gave it to me, and told me to sit and wait until he was ready to perform. He then walked with me, arm in arm, into Second Base and told the attendant that I was his guest. I was seated at a table for two near the stage, and didn't miss a beat or note. I was embarrassed but elated at the same time. Embarrassed because lots of people were looking at me and I didn't think I looked pretty or nice.

After a few songs, just when I was ready to leave, he announced his next song and told the audience that he was going to dedicate it to the woman sitting over there, pointing in my direction. I was so surprised that I don't remember why he said he was dedicating the song to me; everything happened very fast. I don't even remember which song he played for me; I was just so in awe of everything that had happened so far. I didn't stay late as Gary thought I was just going to go ask for an autograph. When I returned and told him what had happened, he could hardly believe it.

Everything wasn't happy all the time, as is the case with all marriages. There were many differences between Gary and me, and I gradually evolved into the person I wanted to be — outgoing, fun loving, and sociable. On the other hand, Gary didn't really want to change. He was happy with who he was, a quiet person who is content with a good book, some classical music, a glass of wine, and a fire in the fireplace. I often felt trapped living that way and wanted to do things all the time. He was happiest spending a quiet evening at home. By the end of the day, he had seen all the people he wanted to at work and was looking forward to a peaceful evening.

So, I went out with the girls while he watched the kids. Of course, this wasn't really the right thing to do, and things became quite tense for a while. But somehow, we worked things out because we wanted to keep the commitment we had made when we got married.

We decided to take a good look at what had happened. The old saying is "opposites attract," and that had certainly been the case with us. I had been 50 pounds overweight when he met me, and he had been 10 or 15 pounds underweight. He was quiet and an introvert, and I was very outgoing when I wasn't around my family. I liked to play my music loud, and still do, and can hardly sit still when I hear it. Gary likes music and prefers classical. I hate it, and so far, I haven't developed an appreciation for it. However, I will listen to it if I must, and shut it out if I don't really want to hear it or go to another room and listen to my music or read.

What has happened over the years is that now I have calmed down somewhat, found some inner peace, and don't have an uncontrollable urge to always be super active. Gary, on the other hand, has come out of his shell and can be quite a talker at times. He also has become involved in volunteering. While we lived in Wisconsin, he volunteered for the Experimental Aircraft Association which he enjoyed as anything to do with airplanes makes him happy.

By the time I was almost 37, I had finally allowed myself to believe that I might be smart enough to study at the university. Before I could change my mind, I signed up at the University of Northern Iowa in Cedar Falls. I had my I.D. and my schedule and was really looking forward to starting the fall semester of 1979. But it wasn't to be. I figured it must have been a sign that I wasn't supposed to study at the university.

Gary had been looking for another job since early spring and had accepted a job in Wisconsin that August leaving me behind to sell the house and move. Hadn't that happened before? This time I didn't have to do any packing and actual moving but it still was a big job and I hated it. I vowed it would never happen again. Next time would be his turn.

The house sold in November, and Hans and I moved in December. Marian was in the Netherlands for that school year. She hadn't known when she left that she would never see her home again. I think it was hard for her initially, but she adjusted well.

We couldn't move into our house until January 1, 1980. I was happy about that because I had plans to spend the holidays through January 14 (Marian's birthday) with her in the Netherlands. She had been without us and far away from home since the middle of July and wouldn't return until the next July. Even though she was living with family — my brother and his family had been kind enough to let her be with them for the school year — she missed her family and friends in the States. So, I promised to come and see her for a month. This meant that I didn't have to do much unpacking by the time I came back since the movers and Gary and Hans had done most of it.

As soon as we were somewhat settled in, I again thought about starting my studies, but doubts continued to haunt me. Finally, in July, 1980, I decided to talk to someone at the University of Wisconsin – Menasha and see what they thought about my dream of becoming a student at my age. They had a two-year program, and the classes were small. This meant that the faculty was available most of the time when one needed help and they really seemed like they cared. I have good memories of that school and would advise anyone who has doubts about their abilities to seek out and enroll in such a place rather than at a big university where the class sizes are large.

I set up an appointment to see one of the counselors about information regarding the school and their programs. I will never forget what happened next. The counselor listened to me and suggested that I just take two one or two classes to start with. Maybe an English class and basket weaving, or art, would be a good way for me to start my next semester. He didn't know about my art ability which was zero. I told him that I had no intention of going at that pace and that I was going to get my Ph.D. in the shortest time possible. At my age I didn't have time to waste. He looked rather surprised but advised me what to do. I didn't have a high school diploma from the Netherlands, but I explained to him what kind of training I had obtained. Even if I had gotten a high school diploma, it would have been in Dutch, and nobody could have translated it.

I was put on probation for the first semester. The counselor suggested that I take a pre-college math class since I had been out of school so long. This meant that I couldn't possibly graduate within the two years I had scheduled for myself. I told him that I was better in math than most high school students and didn't think I needed the class. So, he agreed to let me take a test to see how well I could do. He did the same with English. So, I took both tests and scored very well. I did better in English than a lot of Americans and was allowed to take English 102 instead of English 101 right away.

I could hardly wait for the semester to start. I had signed up for five classes that were scheduled in such a way that I had Tuesday and Thursday off. This permitted me to spend those days at home studying, being with my family, and to save gas. I bought books as soon as they became available and couldn't believe how many I had to buy. I wondered how I would ever be able to learn everything that was inside them in such a short time. Had somebody made a mistake? I asked my neighbor who had a degree from the University of Wisconsin, and she assured me that I had to learn all the knowledge in those books in this one semester. My heart sank for a moment, I will admit. I couldn't see how that would be possible. I looked through them all and read a little here and there, then put them away until I had to open them again. I had to really psyche myself up. I wondered what I had got myself into.

I will never forget the first day of my first semester. I had all the classes I had signed up for that day and was in school from early morning until six or seven that night. I had plenty of breaks in between to let things digest and to meet new people, but these were not easy classes. I had no gym, music, or art classes, even though I realize now that they wouldn't have been easy, either. I had math, English, psychology, sociology, and philosophy. The hardest class for me was philosophy, as most of the material went right over my head. I didn't understand the train of thought. One philosophy spoke about that which you see isn't really what you see or something like that. I wasn't good with such abstract ideas.

I had to work very hard in all my classes, and we did indeed have to learn all the material in those books. I managed to end the semester with a 3.3 grade point average, of which I was very proud. I felt good that I was able to make that kind of GPA. I was so excited that I showed everybody my grades — just like a little kid who gets a good report card. My bubble got burst soon, though, by one of the counselors in the office — an older lady who probably meant well. She told me that my grades really weren't high enough to get into a Ph.D. program. I would have to average at least a 3.75. Fortunately, Gary was very supportive of my grades and our Ph.D. friend Bob told me as well that I had done a great job and to not get discouraged.

After working so hard for almost four months, it wasn't easy to put on the brakes. I remember that we took off for Arizona by car right after my last exam, and I felt lost and empty. Suddenly, I wasn't studying, learning new things, and going at a super pace. By the time we got to Arizona, I had settled down though and was able to enjoy the visit. I did manage to keep up the schedule and graduated with an associate degree with a 3.3 GPA in May 1982.

Since I was still in a hurry to get my Ph.D. in the shortest time possible, I enrolled in summer school at the University of Wisconsin-Oshkosh and took two classes that summer. I would never advise anybody to do that. It was very hard for someone like me who loves to be outside, go swimming, and have fun. But it all paid off as I was able to get my Bachelor of Science degree just one short year later; thanks to the credits I received after taking the placement test for German. I still managed to graduate with a 3.3 G.P.A. I had done the four-year program in three years; not an easy thing to do for most people and especially not for somebody like me who was still struggling with some of the language and who had to take care of her family as well. Gary was wonderful and took over most of the chores and our children helped as well. I couldn't have done it without their help.

Now I had to be accepted in the graduate program, which made me very nervous. I had to take an entrance exam which I kept putting off because I didn't think I could pass. Somehow, I managed to get accepted for the first semester with the understanding that I had to take the entrance exam as soon as possible. I never had the time or wasn't available to take the test until I had finished my first semester. I had done well enough and when my entrance exam results came back, I just barely passed. But since the faculty had already seen how I did they let me finish the program.

I did graduate with a M.S. in Psychology a few years later (again with a 3.3 G.P.A.) and did my internship working for a couple of years in a state hospital in Indiana. I soon found out that being a psychologist wasn't for me as there was too much paperwork involved which took time away from counseling the people. And there was too much politics involved which I didn't want to take part in. When I returned to Wisconsin, I started my own counseling business and did some motivational public speaking.

Initially I had thought I was going to get a Ph.D. in psychology but decided against it for a variety of reasons. I realized that you can change your dreams and that was all right. I never stopped dreaming though and always had something to focus on.

In November of 1994, the day after Thanksgiving, I drove our motor home with our little Geo Metro in tow to Arizona. This was another big step for me as up until then Gary hadn't let me drive the motor home much at all when traveling as we were always in a time crunch, and he could drive faster. Since it was snowing, and the roads were sometimes slippery Gary drove the motor home to the border of Missouri where the roads were clean and the driving would be easier for me. I followed him in our other car. We had decided that I would not drive real far every day as I needed time to find a place to park the motor home and get everything level and situated before dark. I did well even in some situations that could have been dangerous. At one gas station, located below the interstate, one of the attendants started "checking" my tires while I was pumping gas. Gary had told me that I should do everything myself, including checking the oil levels. The attendant had asked me if I was traveling alone, and I said "yes" which is something I shouldn't have done. Anyway, while I was pumping the gas, I had this feeling I better check and see what he was doing. I caught him holding a little Swiss blade knife and he proceeded to tell me that I had a cut in one of the tires of my Geo which might give me trouble and that I should have him put on a new tire and he just happened to have the right size. All I had to do was drive the motor home into the garage and he would take care of it right away. The problem was that once I had done that, I couldn't back out of the garage without unhooking the Geo which was not an easy or fast thing to do. Somehow, I had the feeling that I shouldn't let him talk me into doing that, but at the same time I was worried I might have a flat tire on my trip, and how could I handle the whole situation? I decided to leave the tire on the car even though he said I was taking a big risk. Funny thing is that I drove that car for another two years before we had to put on new tires and never had a flat. So, my feelings were right. I hate to think what might have happened if I hadn't listened to my instinct.

The reason I made that trip was that we had decided that I should move to Arizona to take care of Gary's parents. Over the years they had helped us out a lot when they spent the summers with us and we had promised that we would take care of them when they needed it so they wouldn't have to go into a nursing home. Also, my allergies were very bad in Wisconsin, and I thought the desert would be better for me. My allergist told me that moving to Phoenix would be bad for people with allergies. I had to give it a try as I couldn't leave Gary's parents alone for much longer and we could always move back to Wisconsin, if needed. Gary followed me about nine months later after he retired from his job in Wisconsin. He did have to sell the house this time and make the move. Our son helped load up the truck and drove the truck to Arizona which was very nice. At least we knew where he was and wouldn't have to worry about theft or damage.

Gary's parents died in 1996 and were able to stay in our house with us until the day they died. We still love Arizona but now we want to see more of this beautiful country and our next big dream is to travel in our R.V. for at least a couple of years. We will keep our eyes and ears open for opportunities to stay longer in areas we like to explore more. One way we have done that so far is by volunteering. We have given our time to the Petrified Forest in Arizona and to Arches National Park in Utah. We have found that volunteering is a very rewarding experience which is a win-win situation for everyone involved and we would highly recommend it to anyone who has some time to donate.

Every dream that came true gave me more confidence that not only could I continue to dream, but that I could make my dreams bigger and bigger. I slowly, but surely, gained much more confidence in myself. I know that Gary has been a big part of this as he always, in his own way, pushed me when needed. But I also pushed myself to do things he wouldn't necessarily want me to do but I wanted to badly enough to do anyway.

One of those things was my dream to parachute jump someday. I always admired those brave people and I wanted to be brave like they were, even if it was a one-time experience. So, not long before I turned 55, I decided to just do that. A bunch of people I worked with were going to make their first jump and I decided I was going to go as well. I signed up and charged it to our credit card and didn't tell Gary until just a few days before our jump was supposed to happen. He wasn't too thrilled and wouldn't come along to take pictures of me jumping. He kept wondering why somebody would jump out of a perfectly good plane? He has a private pilot's license and has no desire to do anything like that.

On the day of our jump, reality set in and I became nervous but determined to go on with what I had started. We first had to get some training and it was soon discovered that I wasn't agile enough to climb out of the small airplane and step onto the wing. I had fallen down badly a couple of weeks earlier and I was still kind of sore. I was advised not to do a solo jump but do a tandem jump instead. They had a big plane going up with a bunch of professional jumpers. The only thing different was that a solo jump only was 5000 ft., and the tandem jump would be at 12000 ft. Would I still want to do that? Of course, I said yes but once we sat in the plane I was wondering if I had made the right choice. This plane didn't have a door in it so I could see everything getting smaller and smaller. Finally, we reached the right altitude and it was time to jump. I looked down and got second thoughts. The guy who was to be my tandem jumper was a little guy and he would be behind me. He told me that I didn't have to jump if I didn't want to but if I was going to go, we needed to do it now. I closed my eyes and said: "Okay, let's go." And so, we jumped. I am glad I did it once but don't know if I would do it again. It would have been okay if I had taken a Dramamine because I became very nauseated after the parachute opened abruptly and the guy behind me made some turns to let me see more of the area. I became so limp that I fell on the ground and scraped my knee so badly that it tore up my pants. The tandem guy wasn't too happy about that as he fell also but not as bad as I had fallen. However, that experience hasn't stopped me from trying out different things. I seem to have a need for adventure and as long as I want to, and am able to, I will take care of that need.

As you can see, I have come a long way. Some of my dreams have taken a long time to accomplish, but I never gave up hope and eventually all of them have come true so far. I continue to think of new dreams — little and big dreams. As long as you have something to live for you won't get bored.

PHOTO GALLERY

My husband in his military uniform and how he looked when I met him.

Me and Gary on our wedding day.

Me and Gary at a friend's house for dinner.

ACKNOWLEDGMENTS

Many people have been instrumental in not only the writing of this book but in helping me get to this point in my life. I can't begin to mention all of them. I would like to thank my husband who has been very supportive of everything I have done to become the person I am today.

Many long-time friends have been there for me through thick and thin and have all helped me with their unconditional love. Our friends Bob and Pen have not only been very dear friends, but mentors as well. My friend Helen has been very helpful with her feedback and thoughts after reading my manuscript. I would like to thank each and every one for their continued support and friendship.

I particularly want to thank Tom Chenault, Jordan Adler, and John Milton Fogg who have been key figures in guiding me and supporting me to become the person I am today. Even Wayne Dyer who took the time to respond to me with a personal handwritten letter encouraging me to publish my book.

These people inspired me and encouraged me to keep going when the going was tough. Their books and recordings encouraged me and helped me see that I too could become the kind of person I wanted to be.

ABOUT THE AUTHOR

Françoise Maricle was born two months premature in a Japanese internment camp in Indonesia during World War II. After the war, her family left the tropics they loved to return to a cold, overcrowded Netherlands, where they were met with indifference by the European Dutch. Seeking peace and belonging, Françoise eventually met her husband in Germany and later immigrated to the United States—where she found gratitude and healing.

As a counselor supporting women in abusive relationships, Françoise discovered that sharing her own story created powerful connections. When women heard what she had endured, they became more open to facing their own challenges.

Over time, she began speaking publicly about her life and was interviewed on both public radio and television. Writing her memoir took fifteen years, as long-buried emotions emerged in the process.

Françoise now lives in Arizona, where the wide-open skies and warm climate offer the sense of freedom and peace she always longed for.

www.ingramcontent.com/pod-product-compliance
Lightning Source LLC
Chambersburg PA
CBHW031501120626
46545CB00005B/1693